The Cornflake Kid

Mark Riddell

Published by Partnership Publications

This book is copyright. Apart from the purposes of private study, research criticism or review, as permitted under the Copyright Act, no part may be reproduced by any process without written permission.

© Mark Riddell 1996

Additional copies can be ordered by sending your name and address and a cheque for £6.99 + £2.00 postage and packaging per copy payable to: The Cornflake Kid Book Offer, P.O. Box 131, Bury, Lancashire, BL9 9FA.

Printed in Great Britain by Antony Rowe Ltd, Chippenham, Wiltshire

*Dedicated
to
my
mother*

Contents

Introduction	**1**
Chapter One	**3**
The Early Days	
Chapter Two	**11**
Mum Knows Best	
Chapter Three	**13**
Seeking A Cure	
Chapter Four	**23**
Stranger At The Door	
Chapter Five	**27**
Searching For An Identity	
Chapter Six	**33**
Another Move	
Chapter Seven	**37**
Sea Cadets, Officer Dibsdale and Ant Music	
Chapter Eight	**43**
The Cornflake Kid	
Chapter Nine	**51**
We are the Mods	
Chapter Ten	**57**
On the run	
Chapter Eleven	**59**
Going Into Care	
Chapter Twelve	**77**
STIGMA	
Chapter Thirteen	**85**
Digging my own grave	

Chapter Fourteen   **89**
  The seed is sown
Chapter Fifteen   **95**
  The Holy Land
Chapter Sixteen   **101**
  To be someone was a wonderful thing
Chapter Seventeen   **107**
  Going Home
Chapter Eighteen   **117**
  The Land of Opportunity
Chapter Nineteen   **121**
  On Deaths Doorstep
Chapter Twenty   **123**
  A real job

Introduction

Writing this book has been a difficult and at times a painful experience as it has meant not only opening my own thoughts and experiences to the reader, but revealing a private and personal part of my family life. This includes my mother, brothers, aunts and uncles, and other relatives.

When I actually sat down and began to write, my memories flowed onto paper quicker than I could write them down. There was one question that ran through my mind constantly and that was 'will people want to read about my experiences?' I will leave the answer to this question with you, the reader.

The Cornflake Kid is not about the post war years of Britain, the 'jivin' fifties or the Beatlemania of the sixties. It's about my upbringing, not an average kids upbringing where play and fun are predominant for the first thirteen years. I will admit that I was loved and looked after for the first nine years of my life. The rest was a struggle to gain any sort of care never mind love. It all changed in the space of a year. My circumstances went from bad to worse. After the death of my mother in 1977 I went back to stay with my father. I was very unhappy, but I found a love for music. The words reached out and touched me and at times kept me alive. They inspired my instinct to live. I feel I owe so much to the emerging punk era of the late seventies, and the revival of the Mod scene in the early eighties. It has good and bad times. It tells of my experiences in local authority care and how I was constantly bombarded with rejection and social injustice.

The aura that the book gives off is one of reality and why at times we all find it so difficult to contend with it. We all need to escape one way or another. My problem was when I did escape or shout out I was penalised.

The book moves quickly from the stability and happiness of my life to explore the devastating effects of my family breakdown. The emotional turmoil of my physical separation from family into care. followed by my own self-discovery of new strengths, feelings and experiences.

The book is about survival and my personal growth, contrasting the experiences of the care system and adolescent sub-culture of the eighties, with the development of the thriving community of the City.

There are many people that I owe my life to, and many that have reached out and touched me. The list would be endless so I won't name them as they know who they are. It is to them that I am tempted to dedicate this book, but won't, Instead I dedicate it to my mother who fought for everything her kids stood for, and how she fought to keep alive. This has been passed to me. Thanks.

All names have been changed in respect of individuals being identified and confidetiality.

Chapter One
The Early Days

It was 1964, the heart of the sixties. The place was a club on the beach boulevard. The night was feverish. The east coast of Scotland was known for its unpredictable weather. The weather was not the only factor that brought people together on this night. It was Saturday night. The night when people went out to enjoy themselves, relax and let their hair down. This night is of so much importance to me. This was the night my parents met. The lights were dim. Smoke floated through the air like an everlasting fog. People were standing along the walls like poetic statues. Their purpose in life lay in the bottom of a glass. Their glasses were full of mixed alcohol. The music was romantic, slightly provocative. The atmosphere was electric. Drinks were being consumed quickly. He stood, wearing a suit. She sat wearing a dress. They were my parents, but they didn't know it yet. They met on the dance floor, it was destined to be. They had met! It was ingrained! Was it love, was it lust, or was it purely natural? They enjoyed each others company. He walked her home. Another date was arranged.

A year later they got married. A commitment to life together. My mother, Sheila, was in many ways too good for this world, and my father. The more I got to know the world and my father, the more I believed this. Four years later, I was to be. My opportunity to live. This sperm swam wildly among millions of other sperm. This sperm was strong, fast, and knew where to go. A head on collision was inevitable. All this sperm had to do was get inside. Once inside it had a job to do. To create me. I had a sense of being. I was safe! Questions ran through me from my mind, or was it my soul. Who am I? Where am I? Where am I going? Do I want to go there? I was surrounded by a liquid. I liked this place. It was safe. Each

The Early Days

day was different. I grew more. I became more uneasy about this place. Then one day I felt something. I had felt it before, but this time it was different. I was moving. I was finally going somewhere. Oh well! Let's go! Yee ha! Something was tight, almost trying to stop me. Something was pushing me from within. The tightness was around my neck, then my waist, seconds later it was gone. I felt cold. It wasn't a nice place after all. Suddenly I felt a dying pain. It ran through my body like wild fire. I began to cry. I was making noises. Noises related to pain. The noises I made became distant. I felt there was nothing. I saw nothing, but I knew I was something. I must be.

I felt free, plenty of space. I was still cold though. I was moving again, I wanted to ask where am I? Where am I going? But I didn't know how too. I was put beside something or someone! It was my mother. I felt secure. Her heart was beating faster than usual. This caused a vibration within her body. She was warm and so I felt warm. I felt good, she felt good. I needed, she gave. She gave, I took. A basic understanding was formed. A bonding between mother and son. That's the beginning of my life.

When I was born my mother, Sheila, had already had one son Steven – aged two. From birth to the age of five my memories are vague snatches of going to church and Sunday school. I was brought up a catholic by my mother. I used to enjoy going to church as I sang in the choir and had lots of friends. My father didn't believe in religion so did not come with us. Most of my memories seem to emerge after my fifth birthday for some unknown reason.

Other memories that I have centre around our house. We lived in a tenement block of flats in a suburb of the city. We never really had much, but what we did have we cherished. The focus of attention in the house was the television in the living room. Much like other households. This was where everything was done. We ate in there. Did our homework there. Did our socialising there. The flats were built on a curve in the road. It was quite a busy street. At the back of the houses there was a line of grassed areas which you could hardly call gardens. This was where I spent most of my play days with other kids from the block. We used to play jump the

The Early Days

fence or crush the flower. We loved these games but I am sure the neighbour's did not. We used to dig for worms and eat the dry dirt. Never did me any harm. The only time it did me some harm was when I would journey back up the stairs to our house with my face covered in dirt and spitting mud. My mother would look at me her expression saying it all 'Oh Mark why, oh why do you eat dirt'. Whilst I was thinking of a good answer the face cloth would be caressing my face. Relinquishing the dirt into its fibres and allowing my face to breath again. Seconds later I was in the bath getting scrubbed to the bone and ready for bed.

It was about my fifth birthday that I suddenly realised that I had two brothers. I have no memories of my younger brother being born, or even being a baby for that matter. My fifth birthday party seemed to be a turning point for me. I remember it like it was yesterday. I had lots of presents and lots of friends around. One present I do remember vividly was an ice cream cake. My auntie Moira had bought it for me. She was my favourite auntie. It was a great day but something was missing. My father was not there. He never was. Where was he? I wondered. One thing I did realise was that my mother was always there.

One particular day I remember being woken unusually early. I had heard the word nursery school but had very little comprehension what it meant. Apparently this was where I was going. This was to be my first day and the beginning of a harrowing journey.

She was there first thing in the morning getting me ready for nursery. This new place I was going. Where was it? What was it? Why me? Breakfast was on the table as always. We had cereals, toast and tea to wash it all down. I always had clean clothes. We all did. She walked me to this strange place and kissed me on the cheek. She said I would be alright. I thought, well why wouldn't I be alright. What can possibly happen to me. A last minute tug at my school blazer and a comb through my hair and I was ready to go. Then came the bad bit as she said goodbye. Hang on a second, where are you going I thought. These were only thoughts. I stood with my mouth wide open catching flies and anything that was in range of my mouth. I was speechless and motionless. This is the first memory I have of feeling abandoned, separated and lost. She had left me. I began

The Early Days

to cry. I stood at the school door as my mother waved goodbye from a bus window. I stood alone. A teacher came to the door. She was a burly woman with black hair in a plait and a few moles, which were the talk of the school playground. To her annoyance she earned the title of witch. 'Mark! get inside,' this woman shouted at me. Her voice had no feeling except that of sheer hell. Her voice ran echoing through my body. 'Stop crying, boys don't cry, its bad' she said. I wanted to reply but couldn't. Why was I bad? Because I wanted my mother.

It seemed like an eternity as I awaited lunch time. My mother had told me to come straight home as she would be waiting for me. The school bell rang. I bolted for the door. I ran all the way home and up the stairs non-stop. Through the front door like a bat out of hell. A voice inside me was saying I want my mum. I found her in the kitchen stirring the tomato soup where she was every day. I hugged her, she hugged me. I was safe again. We were reunited. I loved my mum and she loved me.

The separations continued, but I became more accustomed to it because my mother was always there when I got home at lunch time and after school. Everytime the memory emerged of being left alone, I would at times pretend to be sick, but I wasn't. I was worried, anxious and afraid of being left or abandoned again. I suppose in one way or another every kid must go through this; for me it was just natural. In one way or another I had become totally reliable on my mother for security, comfort, love and care.

My relationship with my mother continued to flourish. I knew she had a special place in her heart for me. One good thing about being a mother, and especially my mother, was that she never showed any favouritism towards me in the company of my other brothers.

The bonding between us was solid. Being left alone by my mother was a harrowing and terrifying experience. The feelings of being alone in a school with no familiar surroundings or people I knew was a daunting experience to overcome. The smell of disinfectant, polished floors, cold damp walls and that 'tinge' of school blazer will remain in my nostrils for ever. Walking down the long, lonely corridors that seemed to go on forever will remain inside me as a feeling of isolation. The teachers were nice, well

The Early Days

they had to be, it was their job. They offered me milk and an opportunity to gain preferential treatment in return for me being a good boy. I was bribed into being good. This didn't always work.

I remember one day when my father did come home. He gave off a terrible stench. He was drunk. I remember the expression on his face and his inability to speak. He giggled and laughed. It was the only time I ever laughed with my father.

Again the memories are faint. A few years had passed and I was eight years old. The nearest memory I had of these three years were of being on holiday at Butlins in Filey. I remember trying to play bingo with my grandmother and heard someone shouting 'house'. I shouted the same, minutes later and was told by all the 'old biddies' to shut up – in a kind way of course. I was eventually ushered away with the taunt of an ice cream. I was happy with that.

Shortly after this I remember my mother and father going on holiday to Spain and leaving us with my favourite auntie and the next door neighbour. The next door neighbour was lovely. Her name was Dorothy. She was a very kind, caring and loving woman. They seemed to be away for months but in fact it was only two weeks. When they returned we received lots of presents and sweets.

The days now began to pass very slowly as I started to learn and understand more about the world around me. I feel this was because of my mother complaining of severe headaches. I came home several times to find her huddled in a chair crying. The pain was at times unbearable for her. My father never helped as he was never around and when he was he was too drunk to care. I remember one time he did come home. A huge argument ensued and a lot of shouting took place. I got out of bed to see what was going on, and as I walked into the living room I found to my horror my father throwing a phone book at my mother. I later found out that this was a regular occurrence. I related the headaches and crying to one contributory factor, my father.

At a later date another argument was taking place. This one was different. This time I stayed in bed. In case I got hit by the phone book. Shortly afterwards my mother came into my bedroom. I was still awake.

The Early Days

She said 'we are leaving and not coming back'. These words were said with so much conviction, feeling and determination, that all I could do was cry with my mother. We both fell fast asleep.

This was not the only time when I knew my mum was upset. I remember going to my mum's work with her during the school holidays. When she had finished work we went to catch our bus home. We were standing at the bus stop waiting for the bus in the pouring rain when suddenly I heard my mum sobbing. Her face was in tears. I asked her what was wrong. She said my father had just driven past with another woman in the car. I later found out that he had been having an affair with a woman he worked with for some time. My mother knew this but was waiting for the right moment to leave him.

That night another argument took place. My mother swore blind that he saw us and smiled. My father denied it and tried to say she was wanting rid of him, using any excuse. Again my mother received a beating.

Times were not always bad. It was approaching the Christmas of 1976. I remember it because it had snowed throughout December. It must have been about two feet deep. I also remember this Christmas in particular because it destroyed the myth of Father Christmas for me.

It happened like this. Before going to bed on Christmas Eve, Steven and myself prepared some food for Santa and his reindeer. As per usual a can of McEwans Export, a few mince pies and some carrots for the reindeer. When we had done this we journeyed off to bed. Later in the evening I was awakened by Steven who had put together a ludicrous plan to catch a glimpse of Santa Claus. We both sneaked through to the living room where we anticipated seeing Santa, and hid behind the sofa. We lay there as if we were logs of wood. We dared not move an inch. A short time after we heard the door open. Seconds later we heard the can of McEwans Export being opened and a munching sound. It must be Santa Claus we both thought. We both peaked out from behind the sofa and to our amazement saw my father eating the goodies. We both looked at each other in astonishment and at the same time shouted out 'they're for Santa not you'. My father jumped about three feet into the air with fright and I swear he banged his head on the ceiling. My father offered no excuses for what he had done. Instead he carried on drinking the beer, and we were sent to bed. My dream of Santa was shattered. The myth was gone. This is one of the only pleasant memories I have of my father.

Chapter Two

Mum Knows Best

After that Christmas my mother had planned to leave my father. We were planning to live at my favourite auntie's house. She lived in a small village about fifteen miles outside of the city. It was Friday and the last day of school for the week. I came home to find my mother packing some of our belongings into suitcases and boxes. She beckoned me to put some toys and clothes into some bags. I went to the toy cupboard and grabbed my favourite toys, which at the time were four large combat soldiers, a regiment of Scottish Highlanders and my action man. As I put them in the bag I enquired 'are we going now?' My mother looked at me and replied 'Yes, but don't worry about it, we are going to your aunt's in the countryside'. We packed most of our belongings and put them into my aunt's car. After having tea we all got into the car and drove off. I remember looking out of the back window of the car thinking I liked that house, and that I had forgotten my action mans' tank. A tear ran down my cheek – not because we were leaving, but because I had forgotten my tank.

My aunt's house was quite along drive. We arrived and unpacked our belongings. Then I went out to discover my new surroundings and to meet new friends.

That evening, back at our empty house, my father arrived home in his usual drunken state. There was no-one up to greet him or to decipher his drunken slur and to establish how much of his wage he had spent on booze. He must have thought we were all in bed and for once had decided not to drag my mother out of bed to make him something to food. He decided to have something to eat and put the chip pan on to heat. He then went into the sitting room to have another drink and also to phone

Mum Knows Best

his mistress. Before he even dialled the number he fell into a deep unconscious drunken sleep. He woke a few hours later to find himself engulfed in black smoke and having difficulties breathing. Seconds later he was faced by two firemen in breathing apparatus. They managed to drag him to the sitting room window where there was a ladder waiting to take him to the ground. When he got to the ground he suddenly remembered he had a family and that we were in the house. Little did he know that we had left hours before. He looked up and saw the house alight with raging flames and black smoke. He suddenly sobered up and made an aggressive run for the landing door. He pushed past several medics, firemen and some of the people who lived in the same building. He ran like a madman shouting my kids, my wife, their in there. By this time the landing was alight but this did not hinder my father – he was going in to get us. This may have been the only time my father really cared for us. Two firemen ran after him to try and stop him. But to no avail. He ran through the flames as if they weren't there. Suddenly he disappeared. He was found on the floor unconscious. They managed to get him breathing again and got him to his feet. They could not go back down the stairs, as they had crumbled under the intense heat. The only way down was out of the window. As the firemen tried to carry him my father decided again to try and find us. He struggled free from the clutches of the firemen and ran towards a bedroom. The flames were too much, he couldn't get in. He had to give up, he ran into the sitting room and jumped out of the window. He woke the next day in hospital. He had some burns and a fractured knee. He was told he was lucky to be alive. Our home was burnt to a crisp, there was nothing left. My mother saw it on the local television news. After she had told us, my first thought were for my favourite toys. They were all ruined. This man, my father, was really getting on my nerves. I deeply began to hate him, and it showed.

Chapter Three

Seeking A Cure

Living at my aunt's was great. The air was clean and there was plenty of freedom. Very different from the hustle and bustle of the city. I used to walk along the coast for miles and miles, climbing and walking the cliffs edge. Some times I would take a dangerous journey down the cliff face to the sea. I loved the sea. The smell of the salty air and the noise of the waves battering against the rocks. It was bliss. It was a form of escapism for me. Especially now that summer had arrived.

On most of my quests I would head off early in the morning with some biscuits and crisps just as the sun was reaching its full strength. I used the sun as my guide, pointing me in the right direction. It came up behind my aunt's house and would set in front of it. It was nature's way of telling me the time, or more importantly when it was time to go home for tea. Walking enabled me to get away from the haphazard life of being a child.

A life of never being old enough to watch a late night movie or stay up late to entertain the family. I could walk, think and be at one with nature.

It was a great place. It had a small cove with a pier stuck right in the middle of it. The rocks and cliffs were ideal for fishing for crabs and starfish and for generally getting wet. This was a regular occurrence for me as I loved water. The cove was the shape of a half circle with small fishing huts that stored nets, baskets, small boats and any other tackle that would fit into them. The wind and sea air beating against the huts made them look as if they were hundreds of years old. They possibly were.

My favourite haunt was a cave to the left of the pier. It was a small hole about four feet in height from the outside, but once you were inside it was huge. I found the hole by pure accident one day whilst exploring my new surroundings. At first I was too scared to crawl inside. It seemed to be

Seeking A Cure

neverending. I did at times venture as far as I could but was usually stopped by the intense darkness or the strange feeling that someone or something was watching me. One disadvantage of the cave was that at high tide you could not enter it or leave as the water covered a main stepping stone which helped in the access to the cave. I had to plan my day out around tide times. I sat around timing the tides by the position of the sun and by keeping a keen eye on the rising water on the huge rock outside the cave.

Another favourite place of mine was a small stream that met the sea. It was not very deep but ideal for messing about in. There was a small bridge that allowed you to cross it. I preferred to take the treacherous journey of jumping from rock to rock. The thrill of falling in and getting wet or jumping across and staying dry was more inviting than simply walking across the boring old bridge. On the days when I was in a lethargic mood I would spend most of the day sitting on the bridge with my feet dangling in the water. I would sit there for hours on end with not a care in the world.

On the days when I wandered along the rocks I wasn't a child anymore. I was an explorer on an expedition to a dangerous and foreign land. Everyday was different as I would discover some new land or find some strange foreign object left discarded by some explorer before me. The distance I travelled depended on what was for tea. If it was my favourite 'stovies' – potatoes, meat and veg all mixed – my expedition was always cut short with my stomach controlling my mind. The acids were fighting the brain cells. What was more important food, or thoughtful stimulation? I would say they both won an equal amount of days. The thought of missing out on a second helping of 'stovies' usually swung the decision though.

I remember wandering along the cliffs one day, knowing that 'stovies' was on the menu for tea and suddenly noticing the sun disappearing in front of me and over the horizon. One minute it was there next it was gone. It had dropped into the ocean like a huge coin never to be found again. Possibly lying next to a shipwreck. For once my timing was out. A mistake I usually never made. I knew instinctively it was nearly tea time so I ran like hell as fast as I could, dodging some rocks on the way to the cove, through the small stream past all the huts and up the side of a hill that was a short cut to my aunt's house. By the time I had got home tea was just being served. My mum and aunt thought that I was being chased by the devil. But all I wanted was 'stovies'.

It must have been a few weeks before things began to change. Not a direct change in surroundings or anything, but a change in my mother's physical appearance. I began to see her less often. She spent most of her days in the bedroom. Most of the times I went up to see her she would be fast asleep. I remember several times going into the bedroom to find her lying asleep. She always slept with her hands on top of each other on her chest. In a way almost praying to God. On one occasion I remember watching her intensely for about ten minutes. She looked happy, problem free and in a state of pure relaxation. She did not move or twitch a muscle. She still did not move, but I knew she was alright. I left the room without her even knowing.

Curiosity was by this time getting the better of me. I went downstairs to my aunt and asked her what was wrong with my mum. She said 'She's not very well Mark, and is staying in bed until she's better'. I knew from the tone of her voice that something was wrong with my mum. What was it I wondered? Was it the moving house, or was it me?

Anyway, I thought God would make her better. I trusted the power of my faith and the healing powers He had. I had been brought up to believe in the Almighty, and that a saviour in the form of Jesus had come to earth and could heal people, regardless of their sins. Had my mum committed any sins? She couldn't have as she had been asleep and in the same bedroom for at least a few weeks. I concluded that it must have been me. But what had I done that was so bad in the eyes of God? Was it that I had left my greens on my plate the other night at tea time? Was it that I had left my mum when she needed me most through the day? Was it because I had not gone to church for a little while? I couldn't work it out. I promised I would do more in my prayers and also included in my prayer a cry for help from Jesus or God to heal my mum as I need her and loved her immensely. Over the next few days I thought it was maybe because I had shown too much love for my mother and not enough for God. By this

Seeking A Cure

time my mind was in a complete mess. My direction in life had gone. I was guilty of something, but God knows what.

I remember another occasion, a few weeks later perhaps, going into my mother's room to find her lying on the bed. This was the first time I had seen my mother looking so bad. Her face was drawn and pale, almost as if the blood had left it altogether. On entering the room she tried to focus on the blur at the door. and in a vain attempt tried to move into a position where she could see me. But the pain, turmoil and the agony inside her head was too great for her to do so. For some strange psychic reason, before I said a word she knew it was me. She asked me to sit on the bed, give her a hug, hold her hand and to tell her about my days of exploring. I hadn't had a proper conversation with her for what felt like a thousand years. In reality it must have been a few weeks. I told her about my expedition and my discoveries. She tried so hard to listen and eventually gave up and allowed a few tears to send her to sleep.

From that moment on, my whole world seemed to crumble under my feet. The next day my aunt sat all the family down and explained that my mother was not well and that we would have to muck in together to help each other out and to relieve the pressure on my mother and aunt. The first thing I did was learn to tie my own shoe laces because I felt I burdened my mother with it. I sat on the stairs for hours and hours trying to tie them left over right and under. I could do that bit. That was easy. Then came the hard bit. Make a bow and wrap the other one round it then pull tight. I couldn't do it. After many hours sitting on the stairs I had finally done it. I shouted at the top of my voice and ran around the house like a raving maniac. Everyone thought I had gone mad. This was a great achievement for me and it showed. When I told my mother she smiled at me. This was the first time she had smiled for a long time.

The days seemed to pass really slowly now. Some days were better than others for my mother. Sometimes I would get up to find her in the sitting room having a cigarette. I don't know where she got the strength from to get down the stairs. She would have a cig in one and a cup of tea in the other. The cigs were her only luxury in life. She had very little strength to do anything. A walk around the block was a marathon for her.

Seeking A Cure

On good days when she looked a little better, not very often though, she would insist that she came with me to the pier to get some fresh air. I would take her to my favourite hunting spot for crabs and star fish. We just sat there for hours on end watching the sea. Our trek back to the house was a lengthy one. I could see the struggle on her face. I knew loads of short cuts but they were pretty treacherous for me, never mind my mother.

My mother's condition deteriorated. She stopped eating and spent most of the day in bed. This was when she began to show signs of real ill health. I knew my mother was ill, but not really how ill she was.

It was about the beginning of February 1977. I had been living at my aunt's for about three months before my father came to visit us. He came to take us out for the day. He had brought us some sweets and some T-shirts. The T-shirts were two sizes too small for me, but I ate the sweets. Why not! That showed how much my father knew about us. Well, there was one consolation. They fitted my younger brother. We spent the day at my grandmother's. My father disappeared until it was time for us to return. He took us home later that evening to my relief. I could smell the alcohol as he spoke every word. It oozed out of his mouth just like it came out of the pump in the pub. It was disgusting.

When I questioned my aunt on how my mother was doing she would say that she was getting better and was in the safe hands of God. He would look after her.

My older brother became very unhappy living at my aunt's and longed to live with my father. With a little persuasion from my father it was decided that Steven would live at my grandmother's with him. Within the matter of a few weeks he had moved to our grandmother's. I never really missed him as we didn't get on to well. I was to young to be his mate. He wanted older mates.

Whilst all this was going on I had started at the local school. Much to my disappointment, my days were now in classrooms rather than at the cove. I made some new friends and found some new 'hiddie holes'. I spent most of my time after school down by the stream before going home. Another short cut that I had found was to follow the stream for about half

Seeking A Cure

a mile then head over some wasteland. It was only a short trek from there to my aunt's. That's the bit I enjoyed.

Now that weekends were the only real free time I had, I would go on longer journeys. My mother's illness had prompted me to change from an explorer looking for foreign lands and artefacts left behind, to a doctor looking for a cure for a patient. In this case my mother. I used to wander for hours, picking various flowers, weeds and heather thinking that they may work as a cure for my mum. I used to pick small flowers that grew on the rock face because their colour was a fantastic bright yellow. I would put these into my pocket very carefully and take them back to my mother. I was determined that these would cure my mother. When I gave them to her she would smile and kiss my cheek. In a way they were a cure. They made her smile! This was what kept me going.

My mother's illness had affected my life in so many ways. I was never the same again. I had lost everything. I lost my appetite towards exploring the cliffs for cures. I didn't need a cure – now I needed a miracle to make her well. I used to pray every night to God to make my mum better. I continued to do so for what felt like years of praying. I even began sleeping with my hands on my chest as my mother had. I felt I had done something to annoy God. At first I thought again that it was because I had not been to church as regularly as I used to. I justified this by mentioning in my prayers that whilst moving houses and all that, I did not have much time to spend in church. I had been several times on a Sunday morning but that was all. One thing I did realise that God loves everyone and would not do anything to hurt you or take anything or anyone from you.

My next memory is a few months later. It was about May. I remember it because of the change in the trees and the environment around me. Everything was turning green and blossoming. The flowers were sprouting buds and the birds were singing. I got up early this morning because we were going to the fair with my brother and cousins. We had a great day on the rides and eating hotdogs. I spent most of my money on several attempts to win a small artificial flower. I wanted this flower because I knew it was not real, and that it would not die so that my mother could keep it forever. Looking back I suppose it represented my mother and that

Seeking A Cure

I never wanted her to die. Late on in the afternoon I suddenly felt something inside me. I got goosepimples and could only think of one thing and that was my mother. I told my cousin I needed to get home right away. She said we would go soon. That was not good enough for me. I shouted at her with so much feeling 'its my mother, she wants me'. The look on her face was that of shock. She could not believe my determination to get home. All the way home on the bus I sat as quiet as a mouse. I clutched the flower I had won with all my strength. As I got nearer our house I began to get anxious, my heart was beating fast and I knew something was wrong. As I approached the house I saw a man in the hall. He had a brown bag and some notes of paper. My aunt told me not to go up stairs yet as the doctor was going back up to see my mum. I waited and waited which seemed like a lifetime. He finally came down the stairs with my aunt who saw him out the front door. My aunt sat my younger brother Scott and I down and said that my mum was very ill and had suffered a stroke. She said the stroke had made my mother's face change a bit. My aunt broke down in tears while she was talking. I asked her if I could see her. She said it was alright. I went up to the bedroom with my flower. By now my mother looked very drawn and pale. She had not eaten properly for many days. She couldn't open her eyes or even move for that matter. I told her I had brought her a flower that I had won at the fair. I put the flower into her hand. I saw her hands tighten as she held it to her chest. I sat there just staring at her. I didn't move for hours. A few times my aunt tried to prise me away but to no avail. I wasn't leaving her again for any length of time. I had made that fatal mistake before.

My journeys to the rocks stopped. I spent all my time with my mother. Everyday I came home from school to be there. My nights were spent at her bedside. Nearly every waking moment.

As I strolled home from school one afternoon I suddenly felt that distinct urgency to get home. As I reached the car park I saw an ambulance. No it can't be I thought. I made a dash for the house, but was met by two nurses and a doctor who were helping my mother down to the ambulance. I stood there frozen. The numbness froze my speech. As my mother got nearer I saw she was carrying my flower. She looked at me and smiled

Seeking A Cure

as a tear ran down both our faces. She leant over, gave me a hug and a kiss and said she loved me. She said I would see her soon and for me not to worry. I walked her to the ambulance and tried to go with her, but they would not let me. My aunt went with her. I stood on the pavement until the ambulance had driven off. There was so much I wanted to say. So much I wanted to do. I wanted to say I loved her, but I didn't.

Little did I know this was the last time I was going to see my mother ever again.

It must have been about two days later. I awoke that morning to a very strange feeling. I can't explain the feeling but it wasn't what I usually felt. Something was missing. Something was gone. Something had happened to my mother and I knew it. I asked my aunt, but she said nothing. My aunt mustered us all together. I could tell by the expression on her face that something terrible had happened. Her face was full of tears and grief. The task ahead of her must have been the biggest challenge she had ever faced. She found it very difficult to tell us. It must have been terrible for my aunt. She had lost a sister. To top it all my aunt was the last to know. She read it in the local newspaper. No one had even considered contacting my aunt or even her own kids for that matter. That included my father. We must have been at the bottom of his list of priorities. Another drink was possibly at the top. Finally the words came out. Her words were 'Your mother has gone to heaven, she is in a safe place now'. The words were deafening to my ears. They caused a deafening silence that seemed to last for ever. I asked when 'will I see her again?' 'I'm sorry Mark but you will never see her again, but she will be watching you all the time, she will always be with you, and she will always love you'. she said. These words were terrifying and seemed to make an huge indentation in my heart. I didn't want to believe it. Now I definitely had nothing. My initial reaction was why had God taken my mother to heaven when I wanted her here. I asked my aunt the same question but received no answer. That evening I prayed to God asking Him why He had taken her. Again I received no reply. I cried non-stop for what felt like years. I had been let down by my mum and by God. This was the last time I ever went to church. The last time I would put faith in anyone or trust anyone for a very long time.

Seeking A Cure

The actual memories of getting over my mum's death are very vague. I can't even recall the point when I stopped thinking about her. The point when my life came out of the nothingness must have kicked in by automatic response. After a few weeks I realised that she wasn't coming back. She had gone forever.

Medically my mother had died of a brain haemorrhage. The build – up of years of headaches and the constant pressure growing inside her head. Instead of seeking medical help earlier my mother passed it of by taking large numbers of headache tablets. She had done this for ages. I only found these things out years after her death.

The next thing to happen in my life was the realisation that living at my aunt's would not last forever now that my mother was dead. I knew He was coming to take us away from that beautiful village. The longer He stayed away the better.

Chapter Four
Stranger At The Door

A few days later a man came to the door. I knew this man. It was my father. He was dressed in a black suit. He asked me if I would like to see my mother before she went to heaven. I replied 'Yes'. My brothers and I sat in the car and not one word was spoken. We drove into the city where we got out and walked into the rest rooms. As I approached the door of the room something inside me told me not to go inside. I began to get agitated. My heart was beating twice as fast as normal. I really wanted to see her but something stopped me. I don't know what it was, but it was powerful. I began to cry, but this was no average cry. I was pinned to the wall outside of the room and could not move or speak. My father, aunt, brothers, cousins and some other relatives all went inside. I was left alone outside. I was alone again. Nothing was going through my mind, not even memories of my mother. I thought nothing, but it felt good. Something told me I had made the right decision not to go in. It seemed ages waiting outside that room. I realised this was my last chance of ever seeing my mother again, but I wanted to remember her as she was when she was alive. I wanted the good days, the good memories and the smiles to last for ever in my memories.

My mother was cremated and her ashes were laid to rest in the gardens of Hazlehead.

Shortly after I went to live with my father at my grandmother's. I started a new school and met new friends. My first primary school was frightening because no-one took me there. I went on my own. I settled in well with other class mates and formed a relationship with another lad who sat next to me. He lived in the next block of flats. We went to school together, walked home at lunch time together and also walked home together after

Stranger At The Door

school. Coming home wasn't the same. My mother was always on my mind. When kids asked if I had parents I told them that my mother had died and that my father was looking after me.

In such a short time my life had been totally transformed. I had gone from one extreme to the other. From having clean clothes, good food in my belly and a clean bed to sleep in, to having to wear second-hand clothes from Oxfam, eating stale bread and week old pies. Nothing could replace that tomato soup or the feeling of being mothered. Shortly after, because my father was unemployed I received free dinners at school. This carried a heavy stigma with the other kids because they saw me as poor and laughed at me. As a family we didn't have much. My grandmother paid regular visits to Oxfam and other second hand shops. She bought bread and biscuits that were a few days old because they were cheaper. Birthdays and Christmas didn't exist because we had no money.

I hated the clothes she bought me. They were so old fashioned and outdated. Most of the time they didn't even fit me properly. The clothes always had this mouldy odour about them. The smell didn't do much for my character, never mind the clothes. It was like wearing a large sign on my back saying bought these from Oxfam. When I did complain I was seen as ungrateful. I was supposed to be grateful for everything I received. The other kids knew they were second-hand. But that didn't bother me too much. I spent most of my time playing football with the other kids. I was never really that good when it came to dribbling, heading, tackling and running with the ball. One thing I was good at was slide tackling. This was my speciality. The other kids used to score all the goals and I used to bring down the opposite team players, legally that was.

We used to play on a small patch of grass near our house. One day we walked across to the grass to find some workmen erecting a sign informing use that it was prohibited to play any ball games there. We were devastated. No more football! We decided to continue playing but shortly after received stern warnings from our local bobby. It was strange because one day we could play and the next we couldn't. This was incomprehensible to me. It had no meaning.

Stranger At The Door

We played other games to occupy our time. To name a few were Hares and Hounds, Kick the Cannie – that was my favourite – and British bulldogs.

Even at the age of ten I was into music. I suppose it was an outlet for me. Something to keep me going. I had similar tastes to a lad who lived in the flats. We were both into The Police and competed against each other to see who could get the most records, badges and posters. Obviously he won but I did tell many lies which he believed. Well he said he did!

It was very tight living at my grandmother's. The house was a small flat on the ground floor with two bedrooms. There was my grandfather and grandmother in one room, my older brother in another room. My father, Scott and myself shared the sitting room on camp beds with woolly blankets. The one's that make you itch. It wasn't the greatest arrangement, but it served its purpose to give us a roof over our heads.

I remember one evening when I thought I saw a ghost. I was coming out of the toilet and passing my grandmother's room when suddenly the door opened and in front of me was this woman with no hair. I screamed and ran to get my father. He calmed me down and introduced me to my bald grandmother. I had never realised before that she had worn a wig for years.

There were pluses to living there. I used to sit endlessly listening to my grandfather talking about the Second World War. He was in the Gordon Highlanders. I always remember the story my grandfather told me about a soldier who shot his fellow comrade while messing about with a gun. He said he was in the trenches digging himself in when he heard two soldiers arguing over how to hold a gun straight. My grandfather went over to see what was going on but was to late. One soldier had pointed the gun by accident at the other to show him how to hold it properly. Unfortunately it went off by mistake blowing the other soldier's head off. My grandfather was left to pick up the pieces. He was not very particular about things but one thing that did make him angry was any type of gun being pointed at anyone or thing. He would go mad. He never allowed

Stranger At The Door

guns to be bought at all. If one had been he would have thrown it in the bin.

It wasn't long before my father was offered a property in the same area that we were living in. My father, my two brothers and myself moved into this new house. It was all furnished, carpeted and had some toys and wardrobes. It was the first time I had been happy for a long while. My father had found a job and we had a home help to look after us. Things were beginning to look up. He bought us presents. We began to have good times again.

Chapter Five
Searching For An Identity

My older brother was going through his adolescent stage and was searching for his own identity. He found it in lyrics written by the Sex Pistols 'Never Mind the Bollocks'. I saw a huge change in my brother. He began to wear Doc Martins and zipped up tartan trousers. I saw him one day in the kitchen with two egg whites. He whisked them and proceeded to rub it into his hair. After he had finished he walked past me and all I could smell was egg. I went clean off anything associated with eggs. Apart from that there was now a great shortage of them. They were on my brothers hair and pillow. My brother spent most of his time in his room listening to the Sex Pistols, Discharge, G.B.H, Exploited and any other music that was deafening to our ears. Walking past his bedroom was like passing a war zone. On his door he had written DO NOT ENTER, TRESPASSERS WILL BE CHOPPED UP. He had also got in with the wrong crowd. He hung around with guys who were a few years older than he was. These guys were also into sniffing glue and lots of other things which would get them high. My brother was submerged into the world of eighties punk sub-culture. He was in up to his neck and he was totally addicted to the lifestyle.

I tried hard to identify with my brother, but he was preoccupied with his mates, glue and music. Everytime I met him outside the house he would slap me across the head and tell me to 'fuck off'. Inside the house he never spoke to me. I knew he was sniffing glue, but didn't say anything because of the beating I would get. I don't even think my father had any idea what a mess he had got himself into. My father probably thought it was a phase he was going through. I knew it was deeper than that.

Searching For An Identity

At that same time I had just started my first year at secondary school. I met new friends and made new enemies. I became best friends with a kid called Michael. He was great. We shared everything from money to bikes. His musical tastes were groups like Crass, The Partisans and Theatre of Hate. They appealed to Michael and I. I began to listen to the music and words. Words like anarchy, sex, violence, destruction, collaborator, shaved heads and punk rock seemed to form my vocabulary. Out of school I wore torn jeans, Doc Martins and a Crass T-shirt. My friend wore the same. We spent a lot of our time in indie punk record shops listening to the latest releases. I felt I needed to feed my habit. My habit being music lyrics of course. They were part of my life – they were my life!

My brother and I were searching for our own identities but seemed to get lost in the chaotic and destructive world of punk rock. The music, to me was not just a frenzied outburst of 'pogo' dancing and extremely loud music, but an inspiration to live and learn. It enabled me to express myself through the words that I used and the clothes that I wore. I was making a statement, which in a negative way allowed me to be judged by other people. On the outside I was rebellious, but on the inside I was lost. Lost in an apathetic, cruel, eighties fuck up. My brother and I were becoming just two of the many casualties of the eighties.

I had a lot of anger inside, but no outlet. When I found an outlet I was judged – mostly by adults – as being out of control. Just another kid who didn't appreciate anything. In one way or another people were beginning to take notice of me and listen to what I had to say. All of this had come from listening to music. The music meant so much to me. It continually fed my addiction to express myself. I was changing not only from a child to adolescent but to a human being with feelings and attitudes.

During all of this my family situation began to deteriorate quite rapidly. My father had always been a drinker even when my mother was alive. Nothing had changed, although I must admit when my mother was alive he only got drunk once a week. Now he was getting drunk everyday. He was drinking at work and beginning to spend more and more time as a barfly. This eventually led to him being laid off.

Searching For An Identity

My father was also seeing the woman he had been sleeping with when my mother was alive. He hadn't stopped seeing her even when my mother died. I didn't know this woman and had little intention of getting to know her. This was my opinion, but I knew that if my father wanted to see her or even marry her I would have little say in the matter. This woman could never take the place of my mother and had better not try. As time went on I found out little things about her. My father took one of her three daughters to meet Scott, my younger brother, and myself. My father treated her better than the two of us. He spoke to her more than he ever had with me. This angered me and made me more determined not to like this woman. It also severed the path to reconciliation with my father because of what he had done to my mother. I will never forget that as long as I live.

Perhaps in one way or another, if my father had been a good father, or attempted to be, I would have met him half way. A possible reason for my father's inadequacy towards realising his paternal responsibilities of being a father may stem from my mother's death. My mother may have been the crutch under my father's arm, holding him up whenever he fell and guiding him in the right direction when he got lost. Then when she died he never really got up. Couldn't really face the prospect of caring for three boys. My father needed an escape. He didn't need to look far as it was touching his lips every waking moment of the day. It was the demon drink.

If this was the case, then how could he relate and look after someone else's kids better than he could with us? This was the type of confusion that was running through my mind all of the time. It got to the point that I became self reliant. I almost forgot my father existed. I only looked to him for food or money. If I couldn't get it from him I went to my grandmother's. My attitude was getting worse. It was based on the premise that if I got nothing I gave nothing! I was seeing less and less of my father, and when he was around I avoided him.

I spent a lot of my time with Michael listening to music and staying overnight at his house. I liked staying there because his mum and dad spent most of their time in the local pub, which meant we had the house

Searching For An Identity

to ourselves. The influence of music on us created the idea to play music. We borrowed a lead and bass guitar and practised endlessly for hours and hours. We 'skivved' school to practice. We literally became bedroom hermits.

I schemed this idea to make loads of money. The idea consisted of playing a bedroom concert. We learned five songs on the guitars and asked a friend to play the drums. It was a great idea! We would charge fifty pence entry to the house and plan it for a Friday evening as we knew his parents would both be in the pub. For the price of fifty pence we would throw in some watered down coca-cola and an offer to come to our next gig at a reduced price. We would have supplied some beers, but unfortunately Michael and I were only twelve years old. We reckoned we could squeeze about fifteen people into the bedroom – that's if we put the bed against the wall. It was a revolutionary idea and we could make six pounds and fifty pence after taking out our overheads – coca-cola. We set about making some home made leaflets and distributed them to friends who lived in and around the area. The leaflet informed them to contact Michael or myself. We had a great response for tickets. We planned it for a Friday evening.

As the Friday approached I began to feel important. People were asking me for tickets. I sold all of mine in the one day. People kept asking 'What kind of music are you playing?' 'How long will it last?' and most importantly could they bring their own booze? I told them that they would have to wait and see what kind of music we would be playing, but from my style of dress they had a good idea it would be punk orientated. On the subject of booze I strictly said no to anything that was not McEwans Export. The fifteen tickets that we originally issued sold like hot cakes. We had to hastily make another twenty. The money was rolling in. We planned to do a concert every week for three years. This would give us enough money to buy decent equipment. What an idea!

On the Friday we 'skivved' school by producing two forged sick notes, supposedly from our parents saying that we both had a dose of the 'shits'. The concert was due to start at 8pm as by that time Michael's parents would be well on their way to alcoholic oblivion. Our plan was working

Searching For An Identity

to a dream. Last minute preparations were being made. I played the bass guitar brilliantly. It was a far cry from the harmony of Barry Manilow. I thought I was great and felt like a pop star on stage at Wembley. The concert started on schedule at 8pm.

People were arriving all the time. By ten past eight the house was full. We had a guy called Barry on the door because he was one of the best fighters in our year at school. He was taking the entry fee. We began by playing a track by The Police, Message in a bottle. As we stared our second song Crass, Shaved Woman, I looked out of the bedroom door and saw loads of people drinking, laughing and falling about. This didn't bother Michael or myself, we were just enjoying our fame. Michael was playing the lead guitar and for half an hour forgot it was his house. This was a great achievement for me. It proved I could do anything I wanted.

The entire concert lasted about thirty minutes and was a huge success, although my heart missed a few beats as people pogoed to Anarchy In The U.K. and Exploited Barmy Army. At one point I thought the floor was giving way under our feet. The room quickly became sweaty and packed. I was drenched from head to toe. We received a good response at the end which consisted of people throwing things at us, most of them half drunk cans of McEwans Export. I thought this complimentary because it was a good beer and I salvaged what was left in them so I could taste it. I had never tasted beer before. This may sound stupid as there was so much of it around me with my father. When I did sample the beer I found to my surprise I enjoyed the taste and got a funny sensation running through my mind and body. Come on, I was only thirteen! We finished the gig as planned and began the process of cleaning up. It was nearly eleven 'o'clock and we had to usher the last of the teenage rebels from the house. This would give us half and hour to tidy up the mess, and believe me it was a mess! After we tidied it up we sat down and drank the dregs from some empty cans before we put them into the rubbish bags. We split the money two ways, well three, because Barry wanted a fiver for his services, which we had to agree to or he would savagely rip both our heads from our shoulders. He didn't actually say it but I could see it in his fiery eyes. After paying costs we had made about ten pounds fifty each. It was the

Searching For An Identity

most money I had ever had. I suggested that we go to the chip shop and treat ourselves to haggis and chips, my favourite. On the way down the street we passed his mother and father taking one step forward and three back. We smiled at them and they gave us a pound each for chips. What an evening. We were loaded. We planned another concert for the week after, whilst eating our chips. I slept well that night.

Unfortunately, by Saturday lunch time our dreams and ambitions were shattered. My music career had come to an abrupt end. Michael's mum and dad had received, on top of a hangover from the night before, phone calls from furious neighbour's and a visit from the local bobby. Michael was out with me all day. When we returned to Michael's house he was dragged by the hair and slapped across the head. This was followed by being sent to bed with no tea, and to top all that he was grounded for a month. I was told firmly to make myself scarce in not so polite terms, which I did. The band was finished, my friendship was on hold and to cap it off all my records were in Michael's bedroom. How would I survive with no music to feed my habit? I wandered home in a state of disarray. Luckily he was only grounded until his mum and dad went out to the pub that evening.

Chapter Six

Another Move

Back to reality, at my house problems were rearing their ugly head. My father couldn't pay the bills or buy the food. Partly due to him being made redundant. Slowly he was becoming an alcoholic. Our electricity and gas supply were disconnected. There was no food in the house, and my father was never around, just like before, when my mother was alive. It was a vicious circle and I was stuck in the middle. It was not until Christmas when other members of the family came to celebrate the event that the full extent of the problems came to light.

Shortly after Christmas a family meeting was called at one of my aunt's houses where it was to be decided what my father should do or was capable of doing. The general feeling that he could do very little until he recognised he had a drink problem. Most of my family were there including my brothers and I. We all sat awaiting the arrival of my father. As usual he turned up in his usual drunken state, unable to face the music sober. Our problems were debated at great length for about an hour and things were beginning to get quite heated. The burning question was put to my father what are you doing about your kids? He pulled my younger brother towards him and said 'Steven can stay at my mother's, I'll have Scott, but I don't want Mark'.

Just like that. He didn't want me. What had I done to deserve this? The atmosphere went stale and my relatives were seeing red. My uncle Peter in particular could not contain himself. As a tear ran down his face at what had just been said, he jumped to his feet grabbed my father by the scruff of the neck and hit him several times in the face. Whilst all this was going on I was trying so hard to comprehend what had just been said. The words bruised my heart. My immediate thought was that I wanted my mum.

Another Move

The fight had prompted my father to leave with my younger brother earlier than planned. My relatives were happy to let my younger brother go with my father and for my older brother to live at my grandmother's. I didn't have a home. I was like a lost sheep with neither flock or shepherd. I sat there and cried. My uncle Peter and his wife Pamela said they would be more than happy to have me at their house.

The exercise was to give my father the opportunity to get back onto his feet. A little breathing space. What would happen after that because he said he didn't want me? I took 'I don't want you' to mean for ever.

I went to live with my father's brother Peter, and his wife Pamela. I liked this couple because they were caring, understanding and best of all they bought me plenty of presents. There were only a few teething problems. First, that I had a developed a bed wetting problem!

It was strange because when I stayed at Michael's house I never wet the bed, but when I was at home I did. This problem did not go away and I continued wetting the bed at my aunt's, but not as often.

The other problem was that I had to change to suit their lifestyle. This part I found quite difficult, but after meeting new friends it just came naturally. Living at my aunt's and uncle's was great. I had my own room, plenty of food, made new friends and didn't have far to go to school, which, luckily I didn't have to change school.

My musical interests changed yet again. I was beginning to mellow down from the punk world and its violent way of thinking to an Adam Ant perspective – wearing pirate gear and listening to Antmusic. The lyrics continued to guide me. It was only a change in the way I expressed myself through clothes.

Whilst at my aunt's I joined a local sea cadet unit and had my heart set on a career in the navy. Being in the sea cadets meant I would have to go on courses to different parts of the country. I really enjoyed going every Friday evening and the occasional Sunday morning. I used to get home from school on a Friday and spend at least an hour preparing my uniform. My uncle would then drive me down there for seven 'o' clock. The headquarters were in a few half circle shaped huts. As you walked into the grounds there was a flag mast with the emblem of the unit on it. You were

Another Move

supposed to salute it as you entered the grounds. No-one really did. I must have been the only one who did. I was proud of who I was in the uniform and it showed. Sunday mornings were good because you could turn up in 'civies' and go out rowing down the river Dee.

My commitment, attendance and appearance gave me priority towards going on the next available course. My first course was to H.M.S. Royal Arthur, near Chippenham, one of the best naval establishments to go to. I had saved up all my pocket money, the best of twenty five pounds which was a lot of money to me. I was going with a lad that I got on well with, Steven McKnight was his name.

I remember standing at the train station waiting to board the train. I was standing with my aunt and uncle. Steven was with his mum and dad. I distinctively remember him sobbing and crying, but why I thought, was it me or was it that he didn't want to go? I didn't cry or feel any inhibitions about going. I boarded the train, wet my lips, and kissed my aunt and uncle goodbye. I felt nothing – not even sorrow. The train pulled away and I waved goodbye through a dirty train window which I could hardly see through. I felt free. I was searching again but this time for me, my happiness, my cure, my destiny. I wanted to forget my past, and to find me, my future. My aunt's last words were 'Don't forget to phone me when you arrive'.

Chapter Seven

Sea Cadets, Officer Dibsdale and Ant Music

Before I left I packed my Adam and the Ants tapes and clothes. I had a small tape recorder which I played non stop on the train. After four hours of Stand and Deliver I finally switched it off for about five minutes.

The train journey was direct to London. We had to change in London and get to Euston. For two thirteen year olds that was no mean feat. Anyway we managed it alright. We were soon on the train heading for Chippenham . The train journey seemed to take years. I remember looking out of the window at passing countryside and thinking 'where the hell are we going?' It must have been about ten 'o' clock when we arrived at H.M.S. Royal Arthur. I was so excited that I completely forgot to phone my aunt. We were shown to our dormitory and told to prepare to got to bed.

The next morning I was woken at six thirty and shouted at to get showered and washed. Breakfast was at seven 'o' clock sharp. After breakfast I was ordered to report to the Commanding Officer's office. I could not think what he might want from me so soon. As I walked into the office he erupted. 'Your aunt has been worried sick about you, why did you not phone her?' he screeched in his well trained Army voice. I stuttered the words out of my placid tongue 'I forgot, sir'. 'Not good enough' he screamed at me. I could not get my words out as my ears were adjusting to the loudness of his shout. Then he suddenly exclaimed, 'to top it all she got me out of bed, now that really annoys me'. I tried to say I was sorry, but to no avail and was told to make myself scarce. What a start I thought!

Sea Cadets, Officer Dibsdale and Ant Music

I phoned my aunt right away to save any hassle. I told her that I was too tired to phone the night before, but would phone her tomorrow. I really didn't want to phone her at all. What I wanted was to get on with it. To forget my past for the time being.

During the whole week everyone thought I was trendy as I had the latest musical fashion gear. I also had the latest album by Adam and the Ants. I kept the dorms in music all week.

The camp, as expected, was fabulous. The food was great and the facilities were excellent. Steven and I got friendly with a Petty officer called Dibsdale. After a few days we were getting on really well. He had a bad speech impediment and found it difficult pronouncing his D's. The advantage of knowing him was that he was an officer, which gave him access to certain privileges like alcohol, officers food and a snooker table. It also meant he would not treat us as badly as other cadets.

On the third day he asked if we would like to have a game of snooker on a full size table. We said 'yeah'. He took us to a small unit near the officers quarters. As we were playing pool he produced a bottle of whisky. I think the expectation was that we would be hardened drinkers primarily as we were from Scotland and that we should know a good dram when we saw one. I had never tasted whisky before but decided there was a first time for everything. We drank out of crystal glasses. I honestly thought the life of an officer was not too bad. Apart from introducing us to whisky he also produced some cigars and cigarettes in special boxes. We all smoked a few of each. I didn't inhale as it choked me to death, but it looked good anyway. We were having a great time the liquid was going down like amber nectar. It must have been about midnight when we decided to go back to our dorm.

Dibsdale left us at the top of the road and told us to keep it a secret, which we did. As we walked down the road I could hardly see, never mind walk. I was stinking of drink and cigars. We made it back to our dorm without getting caught. As I got into bed I suddenly remembered where I had smelt the aroma I was carrying around with me. It was my father.

The next morning I woke feeling rather groggy, and so did Steven. My throat was quite sore as well. Everyone was told to fall in the mess hall before breakfast. The Commanding Officer came in with Dibsdale and as always began the shouting. He said someone has been in my quarters playing pool, eating food and even had the guts and bollocks to drink my whisky and smoke my cigars. I want the culprits to come forward or the whole company will be punished. You have until dinner time. I seemed to know what he was talking about but it didn't make sense. I was also still half asleep. His word was law. Who ever did it would be caught. Then it suddenly dawned on me and I think on Steven at the same time as we both looked at each other in amazement. I almost let it slip, but Dibsdale's eyes stopped me.

After breakfast Steven and I were chatting about the incident when Dibsdale came into our dorm. He told us that we would have to own up otherwise the whole unit would feel the wrath of the C.O. Somehow I felt betrayed. I began to shit myself. He also said if we did not own up he would make life hell for us and would also grass us up. We had no option. The best part of it was that he was not to be mentioned. We went to see the C.O. in his office. We told him that we were passing his quarters when we saw the pool table and decided to have a few games. The door was left open so we just went in. On the subject of the alcohol and cigs we just said we wanted to try them. He was frothing at the mouth. He ordered us to run around the camp in full uniform and then 'civies' alternately. We were to do this after tea-time. Just our luck that it began to rain. We were put under the supervision of the gym instructor to ensure we ran around the camp at least ten times. The camp perimeter was about five miles. Our parade dress had to be perfect if it faltered in any way we would have to do that circuit again. It rained continuously all that evening. We got absolutely soaked and didn't get to bed until four thirty in the morning. We had to be up at six thirty. What a day.

One good thing that came out of our antics was that all the camp respected us for what we had done and thought we were sound guys.

The rest of the week on camp went really well apart from the odd dig from the Commanding Officer. I was assessed at all levels of radar reading, radio work, basic engineering, tying knots, parade duties, fitness/assault course, rifle range and of course drinking alcohol and playing pool. On

Sea Cadets, Officer Dibsdale and Ant Music

the rifle range I had scored ten bull's-eyes which gave me fifty out of fifty, the best score in the company. This entitled me to gain my first badges – a star and a rifle.

When we were leaving I visited the Commanding Officer and asked if he believed our story about entering his quarters. He said 'he had heard better'. I confessed the truth to him. He looked at me, smiled and shook my hand. He said 'he respected my courage and loyalty to an officer'. As I walked down the corridor I passed Dibsdale who strangely enough had ignored us for the rest of the week after us confessing to the incident. A few minutes later I heard the Commanding Officer shouting 'Dibsdale'. On the way down the corridor I looked back at Dibsdale who was looking at me. I think he knew what was coming from the Commanding Officer. I ran to the end of the corridor and jumped in the air with two fingers expressing 'up yours'. I had got my own back.

On the train home Steven asked where I had been. I told him I had an outstanding score to settle. He knew what I had done. We both laughed for about an hour at the thought of Dibsdale stuttering his way out of that one.

On my return I felt the burden of living there get heavier every second. I was met there by my aunt and uncle who received me with open arms. I left Steven at the station and said I would see him the following Friday at the Sea Cadets. When I got home my aunt had expected me to have bought some souvenirs which I hadn't. I could see the disappointment in her face. That was all she wanted. I did that course for me not for other people. It was my achievement.

I never really got over my aunt's reaction, and could only feel contempt for her: another relationship that was destined to fail.

I had made new friends whilst at my aunt's and had taken up new interests which included football, table tennis and girls which involved exchanging saliva and playing tonsil hockey, smoking and drinking. I did mostly everything but refused to sniff glue. I used to go out with them when they did but just to keep an eye out for them and to watch for the police. This lasted for about three months.

Sea Cadets, Officer Dibsdale and Ant Music

I knew the consequences of sniffing glue because I had seen my brother getting fucked up.

One night I decided not to go out with them as I was going to the sea cadets. That evening they all got caught by the police and taken home to their parents.

This particular evening was a good one for me as I received a stripe for attendance and a badge for best turned out cadet. I was the talk of the unit. It was great. I felt great.

The next day it was the talk of the whole school that Paul, Dave, Colbert and Ritchie had all been caught by the cops for sniffing glue. These were the guys I hung around with. I was the luckiest bastard around they said. I remember thinking that they might stop now but they didn't. Out sniffing they went and I went as usual lookout.

Chapter Eight

The Cornflake Kid

Residing at my aunt's was short lived. I had been there for about six months. I remember the run up to the day as if it were yesterday. It all started when I heard my aunt and uncle talking about me and expressing how annoyed they were about my bedwetting problem. They both felt that I was doing it deliberately. I think they had based this on evidence that I did not do it at friends' house. The next thing to happen was that my aunt asked me at the bus stop before I was going to school one day if I wanted to go back to live with my father. I told her I did not want too. This was the last thing I wanted. A week or two later I came home to find my aunt and uncle in deep conference. Apparently my father had requested that I should return home as he was sorted out. By sorted out he meant he had another job.

Within a short time, probably a few weeks, it was planned that I would go back to live at my father's, much to my disgust. I felt it was my fault that I was going back. Deep down I knew people didn't believe me when I said about my bedwetting problem and that I could not control it. No-one even thought about the trauma I had been through by losing my mother and all that. It was as if she was forgotten. As if she had never existed. No one ever spoke of her, except at New Year when people were pissed. She was remembered only through the drink. The irony here was that drink ruined her life and mine.

Before I left my aunt's I found out where my mother had been cremated. It was at a crematorium on the outskirts of the city. My reasoning for this was so I could visit her on the day of her death. That was my way of remembering my mother. My way of coping. That was better than trying to hide the real facts as to why my father was how he

The Cornflake Kid

was and how he ruined our family. I always felt that my mother was the scapegoat for my father's problems. The most annoying thing was that people began to believe in my father's innocence.

At the time when I moved back to my father's he was living at his girlfriend's house. This was the woman whom he had been seeing while my mother was alive. My younger brother also lived there with her three daughters.

My uncle dropped me off outside the house, there was a brief exchange of words between my aunt, uncle and myself then they drove off before my father came out to greet me. I was standing alone again on the side of the pavement. How could this man, my father want me now after all he had said. My father didn't even hug me or say anything to comfort me. All he said was 'alright kid'. He took me into the house and showed me where I was sleeping. It was in a single bed with my younger brother. I unpacked some of my things and sat speaking to him for a bit. In the evening I went downstairs with my brother to watch television. Nobody said a word. It was as if I didn't exist. It was like nothing had ever happened. We were all supposed to play happy families. A little later my father said he was going out for an hour or so. Later that evening whilst I was in bed I heard my father returning. He was in his usual drunken state. Within five minutes of entering the house an argument was taking place. The memories flowed back to when my mother was alive. It was happening again. I cried myself to sleep that night. I wasn't crying for my father or his girlfriend, it was for my mother.

Living at this house provided me with loads of scope for my own development. I had come to some adolescent milestones which needed explanations and answers, and believe me living with three other girls under the same roof provided me with some of them. I got on well with the girls and began to notice they were not like me. I knew girls were different in certain ways because of the sex education we had in primary school.

Occasionally I would be in the wrong place at the wrong time. Or the right place at the right time – whichever way you look at things. I would be heading towards the bathroom and would catch a glimpse of a naked body; a girls body. If I saw a body I would go into the toilet and wait for at least ten minutes as I felt this was ample time for them to cover up their parts.

At about the same time, either by coincidence or natural development, I became very aware of my own private parts. I realised that something stuck out under my stomach. I soon realised it was not only for going to the toilet with. I realised that it would grow if touched in certain ways. I had the art of masturbation in my hands. I was very naive about sexual things and had little comprehension what masturbation was for. One thing I did know was that it was enjoyable.

One thing that did annoy me was the fact that the girl's got better treatment from my father than we did. This had happened before. They got money when they wanted it, they got sweets and were able to wind my father around their little finger. This led me to believe that the reason my father didn't want me was because he wanted girls instead. For me it confirmed my idea that this man was only my father because he married my mother.

I lived there for about two months. We were planning to move anytime as the relationship between my father and his girlfriend was getting rather hectic. Incidentally her name was Brenda. She wanted us out as soon as possible. To do her justice she could have put us on the street but didn't. It was just before Christmas when my father was offered a property in a deprived area of the city. My father had no choice but to accept it as this was the only offer he was going to receive.

We moved in on Christmas Eve. We had nothing except a few bags of clothes and two mattresses which my father had bought from a friend of his girlfriend's. Lucky for us my father was still in employment, so at least we had a bit of money coming into the house. Our Christmas was spent sitting in front of a coal fire and living on chip suppers. I remember that year because it snowed really heavily. It was as cold inside the house as on the outside.

In the space of another year I had moved from the comforts of my aunt's house to an even lower standard of living. I suppose one thing I

The Cornflake Kid

continued to have was my music. Maybe I couldn't listen to it, but I could remember it.

By now my music interests had been upturned yet again. I was maturing into sounds like The Jam, The Specials, Madness, Dexy's, and most sixties Mod music. Music again was having a profound effect on me.

The words began to have an impact on me like they never had before. The lyrics expressed to me a world which was by no means perfect, which I could empathise with. Each song I listened to had different attributes whether they were political, violent or oppressive, they all gave me masses of understanding. They comforted me in a different way now, primarily because I was part of that corrupt place we live in. To a certain extent it justified what had happened to me. Life is just like that when you're young.

School wise I was lucky because I never had to change school when I had moved house. It just meant I had to travel several miles to get there.

After Christmas and a quiet, cold New Year, my father did a bit of furniture shopping. He bought a fridge, cooker, two double beds, some bedding mostly woollen blankets, a settee and some pots and pans. All second hand of course. It was a three bedroomed house which enabled us all to have our own rooms. It had no form of heating except the coal fire in the main room. This was home for nearly a year.

My father never really spent any more money improving our living conditions. All that had happened was that my father had no restrictions on how much he could drink. There was no-one to argue with him as to how much he could drink after a night on the booze. He could come home and just fall into a drunken sleep. At the beginning my father was around to get us up for school and to cook an evening meal for us when we got home from it. We would also go shopping with him every week. This lasted for about a month. My father began to depend on me to get my younger brother up for school and to cook ourselves a meal in the evening. Sometimes I wouldn't see him until the early hours in the morning when he would come in blazing drunk. At this point things really began to get worse. My father gave me money to do the shopping every week, pay the household bills, clean the house, feed him when he was around, look after my younger brother, go to school and look after myself. This worked well

The Cornflake Kid

in theory if my father had any money left after drink. I had to take Monday's off school to pay the bills as I reckoned if I kept the money any longer my father might ask for it back when he returned. My daily schedule was to get my younger brother up for school, give him some breakfast and a packed lunch, wash my soiled sheets and get ready for school.

By this time I had developed a serious bedwetting problem. Every morning I awoke to find myself in a pool of urine. It soaked itself into the mattress as most of the times I had no sheets on the bed as they had being washed the previous day and were still not dry.

Going to school was very degrading as the smell of urine always lingered around me. I had to wash in cold water and usually without soap. I earned the nickname 'pishy' and was branded a 'minker'. I had very few friends and so decided not to go to school any more. This was not the only reason. Fitting the schedule of getting my brother up for school, doing the shopping, paying the bills and getting to school myself was too much.

My father was never around to care about how I managed. At times he would disappear for about ten days. During this time there would be no food in the house and we would have to survive on our neighbour's help. To top all this my father got the sack from his job. Now the little money we did have was all spent on drink. The bills remained unpaid. The fridge remained empty and my father stayed away even longer. By now we had to survive on barely nothing. I remember one week when I did manage to get money of my father for food I bought surplus Cornflake's and sugar. The reasoning behind this was that we would have something to eat when everything else ran out.

As anticipated my father disappeared for about four weeks. We only had Cornflake's and sugar left. I knew that Cornflake's were good for you and that sugar provides you with energy. This was the basis of our survival for nearly a week. I would put the Cornflake's into a frying pan with a touch of water and loads of sugar. At first it was very tasty, but after having this at every meal for about a week it began to wear off. When the Cornflake's ran out and neighbour's had been approached for money for chips we were at a loose end. We did not eat for at least a week.

The Cornflake Kid

While all this was going on we had our electricity cut off and letters from Housing saying we were in rent arrears. Eviction was on the cards. To top it all, I was generally expected to go to school, but found it impossible as I had to be around when my younger brother came out of school at lunchtimes as he had no lunch and nowhere to go. I had no lunch to give him.

By now my father had been away for about three weeks. We were both starving to death. It got to the stage where I almost collapsed from lack of food. I was only saved by the sheer luck that a friend we knew gave us some bread he had taken from his house. This kept us going for a day or so. I found it difficult to swallow the bread and had to resort to finding another source of food. This was when I decided that I would steal milk from people's doorsteps. We lived on milk for weeks at a time. This was short lived because people started cancelling their milk or setting traps for me to get caught. That avenue was sealed off for sure. No more stealing milk. Breaking point was slapping me in the face. Things went from bad to unbelievably worse. It was like Nightmare on Manor Avenue. This was the street we lived on. The area was notorious for being deprived. Everyone had nothing. We had no heating, no electricity, no hot water, no food, but what put the nail in the coffin was the flood we had.

It was not really a flood, more like the whole of the street pumping its raw sewerage into our bathroom, kitchen sink and any other crevice it could find. I came home to find the bath overflowing with shit and urine. We did not have much carpeting, but what we did have was surely ruined. The sewerage flowed like a river through every room, finally finding solace in the back bedroom. It must have been knee deep at one point. The workmen from the council apologised for any inconvenience. This was an understatement. How could anyone apologise for that mess? All I wanted them to do was to clean it up. They said they would be back, but they later found out that our house was an imminent eviction case so they never bothered. I tried to clean bits and pieces but got to the point where I was being physically sick. I left it to dry. My father was the lucky one as he had done one of his disappearing acts. After a few days it slowly subsided through the floorboards. The carpets turned a funny brown colour then

The Cornflake Kid

went crispy. At one point you could have gone skidding down the hall and possibly broken a world record. Our bathroom had been a white enamel – it was now a permanent tan colour. We never did get it white again! My brother and myself got stomach bugs and bad headaches for a good while afterwards.

A couple of days later my father returned to find an unbearable stench creeping under the front door. When he opened the door he could not believe what he saw. We had sprouted a vegetable garden in our hall. The living room was like a greenhouse with moss growing up the furniture. The back bedroom was like a marshy swamp. He thought we had been bad boys. It was only when mushrooms and slugs emerged in their thousands that I had finally had enough.

As the next giro day came around I could see my father getting agitated. Drink was on his mind. He could not wait for the next fix to be pumping around in his blood. The demon drink had taken over his life.

The shit we lived in did not seem to matter to my father. He knew he could get away.

The condition's at home never really improved. My father disappeared again into a drunken oblivion only to return when reality slapped him on the face. Was reality so hard for him? Possibly!

On top of all that was going on I had to continue to look after my younger brother. I had to get him to school, cook him the appetising meal of Cornflake's, sugar and water, and make sure I was at home to let him into the house after school. This had several meanings for me. First, I could not get to school myself because the school was at least an hour walk from our house. I had to walk as bus fares were a non-existent luxury. In my eyes my younger brother was my priority. I think during that year I spent about three weeks in school.

Chapter Nine
We are the Mods

During these hectic times only one thing that kept me going, music. I was nearing my fourteenth birthday and was heavily into the Mod scene. Despite our bad living condition's I always managed to salvage the odd piece of clothing or record from the few pounds my father had not extracted from me. I either borrowed or swapped from other Mod friends, or went to the extreme measure of not paying a bill some weeks. My father never knew I did this. Most of the times when I did this it was a matter of urgency. New shoes or something like that. The Jam were my favourite group at the time. I tried very hard to keep up appearances, especially trying to conceal my bedwetting problem. But at times this proved very difficult and on more than one occasion I decided not to go out but to stay in for the evening and stink in my own self-pity. The thought of being outcast by my highly regarded Mod friends would prove too much if it happened. I was proud of the statement I was making when I was a Mod. It was not because of the 'in crowd factor' or so much what I aspired to be, but merely the basic fact that I had something I actually liked and something that I stood for. People saw me as something. This was not always in a good sense as some people did take the piss. Most of the time this came from other adults who for some strange reason had forgotten their own pasts. Forgotten that they had once been teenagers. Forgotten to give the kids of today a chance in an adult world of tomorrow.

The Mod discos were usually the highlight of the week. Any other times we would hang about shop doorways in the centre of town to discuss forthcoming parties and battles with rival Mod gangs from other parts of the city who were frequent invaders of our patch – the town centre. It was also a good source for stolen goods, drug and alcohol contacts. The disco

We are the Mods

we frequented was called St Kays. It was an old church that had been converted into a sort of community centre.

Every Saturday, as planned, we would stand outside our local off-licence and haggle with someone passing-by to go in and purchase our cider for the night ahead. They would not sell it to us as we were only fourteen years old so we got someone else to buy it. Once it was bought, sometimes this process would take several hours, we would consume the alcohol as quickly as possible through a straw for maximum effect. After this we would stagger to the disco. As we approached it we needed to look sober or we would not get in. Once inside you could do whatever you liked. Depending on the state of me, I spent most of the evening dancing nutty style to Madness, 'ghostly' to the Specials and pogoing to The Jam. Unfortunately the disco finished at half past ten sharp. By the time we had been forcefully helped out of the front doors. We were all ready to take on the world. Maybe not the world, but the local biker gang! It was time to go biker bashing!

I despised these leather clad rockers. I was taught to hate them. They were my enemies. I knew that they thought the same about Mods. It was either me or them. I decided to protect my own interests.

That night, like many nights, we headed for the beach boulevard which was their local meeting place. I was uneasy about going to the beach as it was unknown ground, not just to me but to the thirty of us who were going there. It was a good mile from the centre of town which we knew like the back of our hands. We knew every hiding place, every short cut and every dead-end. As we neared the cafes where they congregated I could feel the adrenaline pumping through my veins. My level of aggression began to lose control. My heart was beating twice as fast. Like the rest of the Mods I was ready for anything.

As we turned the final corner they were in our sight. There were at least ten of them. Probably in the region of mid-twenties and as usual dressed in their black leathers. As we approached them we began to sing 'We are the Mods' repeatedly. This gave them the opportunity to face us or run. After several verses of song an attack of the remaining hard nuts ensued. I was in the middle ranks surrounded by nutters in front and shitbags at

We are the Mods

the back. It all seemed to happen really quickly, punches and kicks being thrown at random. I landed a few on someone's head. To this day I am still unsure as to whether it was a biker's head or one of ours.

After our frenzied attack we would head up the 'toon' to boast about our biker bashing session.

The Jam had a profound effect on my life. I lived for the words. Paul Weller was my idol. I needed an idol. I remember when Going Underground reached No 1 and it was played all over the country and on Top of The Pops. I cried that day. When songs like 'Its too bad, 'When you're young' and 'Funeral Pyre' were released I listened with vibrant anticipation.

As Paul Weller was my idol I needed to feed my habit of trendy Mod clothes. I needed a pair of bowlers, Jam shoes, levi jeans, a Mod parka and a boating blazer. I managed to pilfer little bits of cash here and there from my father. I slowly bought the various items of clothing. As my commitment as a Mod increased and my hatred for leather clad biker's grew, I became part of a Mod revivalist group called Scooters Inc. The were dedicated Mods. We would meet on a Thursday evening and Saturday all day at a cafe. We listened to Mod music and filled our coke cans with cheap vodka. I was only fourteen at the time and still living at home – well sometimes! Most of my weekends were spent in the city centre and in the evenings I was at parties.

We were quite a big group – about one hundred. When I joined Scooters Inc there were about fifty of us. We were the elite Mods. To join I had to wait at a set of traffic lights until a biker stopped at them then kick him off and have a go at him without showing any mercy or fear. I suppose it was like joining an old Etonian public school or a fraternity. I showed no fear in doing so. My adrenaline was pumping around my body at a thousand miles per hour. In this instance the biker got up hastily and sped off to gain support from his other smellies as we used to call them. The biker's came in force, but nothing to match us. As we saw them coming up the high street we charged at them. There must have been at least a hundred of us by now. I was at the front with the big boys. I was quite big for my age. I looked about seventeen. I was dodging cars and

We are the Mods

buses. Others were not so lucky and got knocked down. It was a mad frenzy. I loved every second of it. It just so happened that I got hold of the same biker I had kicked off ten minutes previously. I remember punching him and kicking him. He punched me right in the face. It hurt. There was blood. I felt no pain. He didn't hit me again! Minutes later I heard police sirens and we all ran in different directions like ants in a mole hill. We hid for about ten minutes then like homing birds we headed back to our meeting place, the statue.

It was a statue right in the middle of the city centre. We talked of victory and of course my entry into Scooters Inc. I was the talk of the town for a week or so. I was webbed into a culture, a craze, a feeling, an expression. To be someone is a wonderful thing: these Jam lyrics meant it all to me.

My whole attitude and personality was changing rapidly. I was taking it home with me. My father never noticed and was never there to listen. He never really cared.

I had been looking after my younger brother for nearly a year and a half. I had also not been to school for a long time. I remember getting my report and attendance card through the post. I had been to school twenty two times out of the whole year. I never sat any exams. I was in my third year at school. The school's truant officer had been to our house several times to see my father and to establish why I had not been to school. Before he would arrive my father would say to play their game and to say I had been 'skivving' school. He would give me a bollocking in front of the officer with the affect of sending him away feeling as if he had accomplished something with us – a working class family. After he had gone we would have a good laugh.

A week or two later It was a Friday evening and we had all been invited to a party on the Saturday. I had no money and badly needed to go to the party. I went home, took my father's record collection and sold it for a 'tenner'. Come on – they were only Rod Stewart, Tammy Wynette and Sydney Divine. Little did I know they were originals. My father said once they were worth fifty quid each. A slight exaggeration I suppose. I went to the party and got absolutely paralytic. God knows where I slept. I woke up on the floor in someone's house. I got up, brushed my sta-pressed

We are the Mods

trousers down and put on my Mod parka, drank some left over's in a lager can and left. The house was totally wrecked. I couldn't give a shit!

Chapter Ten

On the run

When I got home I knew something was wrong because my father was sober. He had noticed his records were missing because he was planning to sell them, but I had got there first. Not only had he noticed this, but he had found a bag of magic mushrooms under my bed. He didn't know what they were and had flushed them down the lav. He looked at me, and in a vain attempt hit me across the face. It was the first and last time my father ever hit me. It was more of a wasted slap really! He sent me to my bed. I went to my room gathered my Mod gear and left via the window when everyone was sleeping. I wasn't leaving because of the slap, it was a combined thing. I felt I had put up with enough. It was time to break free. I was journeying into the unknown. I went to my friend Keith's house. He would put me up for a bit. His mother was really nice and always seemed to wear short skirts and tight blouses: little did I know she was a prostitute at the time. She said she would like to adopt me, but I think she just wanted the family allowance money. But apart from that she was very nice. I lived with him for a few days.

After a few days I decided to move on. I slept in various sheds and inside flats that were disused. After about two weeks I saw a news bulletin on T.V. in a friend's house. It was me. I had finally been reported missing. I stayed at Keith's and kept a low profile for a few days.

It got to the stage where I needed to get out of being in hiding. I felt as if I was in exile. I needed fresh air. I went to the local shop with Keith where I must have been spotted. We went back to his house. He lived in a third floor flat. Minutes later there was a knock at the door. I ran into the bedroom and hid under the bed. There was no-one in at the time apart from us two. Keith's mother was out on the 'game'. It was the Police.

On the run

They barged in and said they were searching the house. As the bedroom door opened all I thought 'was I am not going back to my father's'. I then heard a voice 'hey come out from under there'. I tried not to move and pretended to be a suitcase under the bed. I then felt a tug at my feet. I was caught. I was nicked. The Police escorted me down the stairs but half way down I decided to do a shoot for the back door. I ran for my life, straight out of the back door right into a black uniform, 'Now, now sonny' he said as he grabbed me by the scruff of the neck. I was then thrown into the back of the Police car and driven to a Police station. On the way there we passed some of my school mates. I waved to them thinking I was 'Archie Knox,' – A statement people use when they think they are great. When I got to the police station there were a thousand and one questions. Where I had I been? What was I up to? Who did I stay with? My reply was I am not going home. My aunt Harriet, my dad's sister, came to pick me up. I went to live with her. This was about mid-October.

A social worker came to visit me. The same one who visited us at home. Two weeks later I attended a children's hearing with my younger brother and father present. It was decided that my brother and I would be received into local authority care. We were to move just after New Year.

While living at my aunt's house I palled up with Keith who had harboured me whilst on the run. I was the talk of the school for a good few weeks. While hanging around with Keith, I was introduced to various types of solvents – gas, glue, thinners. We tried them all. Sniffing allowed me to get away from all my problems. Whilst under the influence I was someone I wanted to be. I could be anyone by hallucination – strong, powerful and at times invisible. I had a good few months! I am sure my aunt knew I had been sniffing but she never said. I used to go straight to bed when I got in the evenings. The smell must have travelled through the house but she never said anything.

I suppose the thought of going into care was a better option than going home to live with my father. In a way I was relieved that I was going into care. My only worry at the time was about some of the stories I had heard about care. In a sense I knew it might be a hard life, but what the hell, my life had been hard enough until now.

Chapter Eleven
Going Into Care

It was the 4th of January – I remember it well. It was a dry frosty, sunny day. The social worker was picking me up at noon. My younger brother was picked up first from my other aunt's with whom he had been living. I remember getting into the car after saying goodbye to my aunt, uncle and cousin. I put my one bag into the back of the car. This was all I had. Some clothes, my record collection and some bits and pieces. We had left lots of things at my father's. Things I knew I would never see again. The opportunity to pick up some other belongings had not arisen.

We both had no idea where we were going. The air in the car could be cut with a knife. I remember looking at my younger brother and seeing sadness and an expression of pure bewilderment on his face. For a ten year old it was probably one of the most frightening experiences to possible.

Me,? well, I was full of anticipation! I could only imagine it being better than living at home in that hell hole.

We drove to a suburb on the south side of the city. By this time I had vivid images running through my mind-barbed wire fences, locked rooms, warders, no privileges, no freedom, etc. But when we pulled outside this average looking house I became totally confused. This isn't a children's home I thought! We both got out of the car, picked up our bags and like two orphans walked behind our social worker to the front door. We were met by an older man and woman. This was the boss and his wife who ran the home. They were of the old school of social work. His principles laid rest on 'I am the warden and you are the underprivileged, I am in control'. Once introduced we were shown a room which we both would have to share. We both sat in the room alone whilst our social worker sorted out some other formalities. My brother broke down and wept. I comforted him reassuring him we would be alright. We spent most of that day in our room. We met the other kids who seemed friendly enough. We both had an early evening. As I was slipping into a deep state of unconscious sleep I could hear my younger brother crying.

The home itself was very presentable, but it had that institutional feel about it. The toilets were painted in blue gloss paint which reminded me of hospitals. It had a cloak room where our jackets, coats and shoes were to be kept. We all had a hanger each. The kitchen was pretty modern and very well kept. I sort of liked this place after first impressions.

The next morning I was awakened by a face I had not seen before. It was pretty frightening at first. This was another staff member. I had also awoken in a dry bed. I couldn't remember the last time this had happened. It was sheer bliss.

The next few weeks that followed were taken up by getting used to our new environment, making new friends, trusting people, eating plenty and worst of all going back to school. I had actually spent one week continually in school for the first time in I don't know how long. This was an achievement for me.

I gradually began to see that people did care about me, but I had this feeling that it would fade like it had done in the past. As I began to respond to the care that I was now being offered, I was allowed a room to myself. I was the oldest kid in the home at the time. I had my own privacy. I was treated as per my age. I was listened to. But best of all, I was given a small record player and some money to buy some records – accompanied by staff of course. I was not at that level of trust yet where I could be trusted with money. That had to be earned.

My room was beginning to take shape. I had posters on the walls and good sounds. My first record was Sound Affects by The Jam. I played it until it wore thin and the staff had heard it thousands of times – and could recite the words perfectly.

My social worker visited only a few times, and when she did it was usually to inform us that my father was coming to visit us the following weekend. We had little say in the matter, possibly because of the chances of us going home, and obviously social work ethics. As the weekend neared my behaviour began to change. I couldn't control what I felt towards this man. I began to take it out on staff, usually shouting or refusing to do certain things. They knew it was because my father was coming. They knew how strongly I felt about my father and that I was adamant that I was not going home.

On this particular day my father was due to arrive at twelve noon. It was a Saturday. Anyway, he arrived at 3pm, pissed out of his head. He could hardly stand or walk. We spent an hour in our pool room. We played a few games of pool and listened to my father promise us all sorts of toys, games, bikes, anything we wanted. I could see right through my father, buy my younger brother was pulled into his web of drunken lies. As my father left, he said 'you won't be here for long I'll get you back'. Little did he know I was never going back. Ten minutes later he was probably back in the pub drowning his promises. My younger brother cried for a while whilst I forgot even seeing him. That was it for another few months, hopefully.

Back at the home it was beginning to get hard work. There were so many people looking after you. So many giving different messages or advice. So many caring about you. At times it was overwhelming, to the extent that I didn't know who to trust or who I could talk too. It wasn't easy. The other kids were so messed up, some were uncontrollable and violent, but there were good reasons for their behaviour. Many had been abused either sexually, physically or emotionally, and some all three. We all had different problems, but our behaviour was similar. In one way or another all we wanted was our mother. Someone to cuddle us, love us, be there for us. This wasn't on offer. We were all being deprived. Only one thing could help us now and that was our own development.

My development was in place, sitting in limbo, waiting for a kick. What my mother had done with me when she was alive was ingrained. Her morals, beliefs and her strength to survive were innate parts of me now. I was lucky because I had a good upbringing. The other kids were not so lucky.

Going Into Care

I was nearly fourteen. As I was older I used my own personality and character to bring around some of the other kids. I took them under my wings! One youngster, Chris was his name, was heavily into sniffing gas and Tipp-EX. He was nine years old. I caught him sniffing a solvent in our local school playground. I took it off him and clipped his ear. On the way back home I found out more about him than the staff had ever done in the time he was there. This was between me and Chris. He told me the secret to his life. He also told me if he had one wish in the world it would be to be at home with his mum and dad. Was this too much to ask? Regardless of the abuse, he still loved his parents. The only difference was that they didn't want him, ever!! He had told someone of the abuse he was suffering, he had betrayed his parents. This was unforgivable in his parents' eyes.

Although I tried to help Chris his behaviour continued to deteriorate. His problems grew bigger within himself. Was he past the stage of help? The home could hardly contain him. In some ways this was doing him an injustice. He needed more boundaries.

One of the other kids who came to the home when I was there was a kid called John. We called him Slim. He was about twenty stone in weight. He was huge. He had come from a special school on the outskirts of the city. Initially he had come for some respite, but for some unknown reason he came to stay permanently. Apart form his size he was quite tall. He had ginger hair and a sweating problem. Generally he was a likeable kid. Well for the first two weeks or so anyway.

I remember my younger brother coming to me and telling me that Slim had tried to touch his private parts. My brother referred to his private parts as his cock. At first I thought my brother was stirring it a bit as Slim had become unlikeable. The other kids were a little afraid of his intimidating size. I decided not to mention anything but asked my brother to let me know if he did it again. I didn't have to wait that long as George had mentioned it to me. He said he was forced into the bathroom and Slim had put his hand down his trousers and had started playing with him. Poor old George, he said he actually enjoyed it, but knew it was wrong.

Going Into Care

Slim had offered him sweets to keep his mouth shut. George came to me in confidence.

By this time I was ready to explode. I did what I felt was right and told the staff. They told me to leave it and that they would deal with it. I heard no more about it.

During this time we had two new kids into the home. David and Anthony were their names. It was funny because I knew them through my father, who knew their mother. They were both drinking partners. We had been introduced a couple of times and had been to their house which was actually worse than ours at the time when we were living in Manor – the area where we had the flood.

They were two decent kids whom I felt would benefit from the care system. One other ironic thing was that David never wanted to go back home, but Anthony did. The same scenario as my brother and myself. Within a few days they had settled in quite well.

On one particular day, Anthony came running downstairs into the small pool room crying his heart out. Eventually, when he had calmed down he disclosed to us that Slim had come into his bedroom and told him to take his pants off. Which he did because if he didn't Slim was going to beat his head to a pulp. Slim pulled his pants down and with one hand played with Anthony's dick while Slim forced Anthony to play with his dick. After this, Slim told Anthony to suck on it which he refused to do and came running down the stairs to us. Before I could respond David was halfway up the stairs to kill Slim. I was in hot pursuit behind him to pick up the pieces. This was not my battle. I was the referee. Although I knew David could handle himself I was there in case he got beat. By this time the staff had realised something was going on and were not far behind me. David booted Slim's door open and gave him a good few punches to the face which Slim absorbed without any effort. Slim responded by going bezerk. He picked up David and threw him across the room. Just as I was about to step in the staff pushed me out of the way so they could break it up.

Slim was taken to one room and David to the office. About twenty minutes later David emerged from the office crying. Slim on the other hand was sent to bed. The staff knew now that there was a problem and that something needed to be done to protect all the kids. In the midst of all this Anthony was only asked what had gone on between Slim and himself. Anthony told them the truth. On the surface of it nothing seemed to be getting done about it. We had a severely mixed-up kid living with us. That was the last I or anyone heard of that incident. I am not sure what went on behind the scenes in the staff room. That was confidential.

This was not enough for me. I planned to get Slim back for what he had done. This was not the only incident involving Slim. A few times I had caught him steeling food, money from our rooms and pockets, and continually masturbating in corner's whenever someone left a room.

One day I asked Slim if he would like to go to the park with me. The park was about a ten minute walk from the home. I promised him an icecream. As I was leaving the staff told us to behave ourselves, especially me. I always did behave myself. That was a funny statement to make. In a sense I knew what they meant: Don't do too much damage to him, and help him if he accidentally falls over.

When we reached the park I bought him the icecream I had promised. We walked around the park for about half an hour when I mentioned to Slim the playing with cocks business. He said 'he could not help himself and could not stop himself from doing it: before he realised it he was doing it'. I asked 'if he fancied any of the kids' to which he replied 'yes'. I asked 'if he fancied me' to which he replied 'yes'. The next thing I knew he had headed away from me towards the bushes. I followed him. He went into the bushes and emerged a few minutes later with his pants down and his cock in his hand. He was heading towards me. I shouted several times for him to pick up his trousers, but he didn't. There were people all over the place watching this going on. I walked away in disgust. Slim followed a little behind me. I kept a look out of the corner of my eye in case he tried anything with me. I turned and said 'alright, Slim you can have me'. We walked a little further out of the view of any onlookers. We went down the side of the pond which was there. As Slim approached, still holding his dick, I said, 'well let's see it you fat bastard'. He moved his hand away and at the same time I lunged forward and kicked him right between the legs. All I heard was his bollocks hitting his adam's apple and the ringing

Going Into Care

of bells – or was it balls? It was done. My opportunity to get all the kids revenge on Slim. I walked home feeling great. I knew I would possibly get shit for this but I didn't care. I walked into the home and was asked where Slim was. I said 'I had left him at the park eating icecream'. I am sure the staff knew to expect an injured Slim on his return. Slim returned about twenty minutes later and went straight to his room. Well he limped to his room. The following day he was in the office asking to go back to the other home or back to his father's. In the following days no-one spoke to him. Soon after that he was moved on, I think to his father's.

The home seemed to settle down for a bit. We got a few more kids in but none as disturbed as Slim. One of the kids we got in was a lad called Bruce. He was different. He was Downe Syndrome. The strange thing about Bruce was that he was treated the same as us, although it was obvious he was not. It was never explained to any of us why he was different. It was like he was different because he was. The other kids took the piss out of him nearly all the time and at times Bruce loved the attention.

After a few weeks of him being there we planned to go on a day trip to Edinburgh Zoo. I volunteered to look after Bruce. A hard task to take on board. On our arrival Bruce and I walked in front of all the others, so we could think I suppose!. We walked around for about an hour until we reached the monkey section of the Zoo. Bruce thought these animals were fabulous. He ran in the direction of the cage entrance. I followed in hot pursuit behind him. As he neared the cage he attempted to climb over it to greet the animals. What he failed to notice was a sign saying these animals were quite dangerous. I went to get him off but he wangled free and ran away to try to gain access somewhere else. Luckily there was no other way in. Instead he ran like a monkey and imitated their sounds. At first it was generally funny until he started jumping onto people. I again chased him, which in turn, made him worse. You can imagine the scene. One kid acting like a monkey and the other shouting after him 'Bruce!,' in a high voice. At first I thought the staff would have intervened, but for some reason I had lost them. Where the hell were they I thought? By this time I was getting annoyed and contemplated leaving Bruce to his own

Going Into Care

devices, but I knew I was responsible for him. I eventually bribed him into calming down with an icecream. I've used these tactics before, but in a different way. The icecream served its purpose, but the downfall was that he wanted more and more. If I didn't he said he would run off again. So for about a few hours until we all met up at the cafe again I had bought him twelve icecream cones. I had spent about ten quid on icecream. I was gutted. I had no money left.

When I met the staff they had no idea what had gone on for the past few hours. They asked if we had a good day. I responded by saying its been fucking unbelievable. After this I mingled with the staff until it was time to go home. On the way home we had a Chinese meal. Bruce fortunately had exhausted himself and had fallen asleep. My first time all day to get some piece and quiet. For the first time I realised how demanding the work must be at times for the staff.

Things went rather smoothly for a few months until I got the opportunity to go and buy some new clothes. This was one of the many instances when being in care was a realism that I was in care and that I was just an object in the whole fucked up system.

I wanted some new Mod clothes. There was only one snag the clothes had to be bought using an order book. This in turn meant no real choice of clothes because we had to use certain shops. When I went shopping I refused to buy any clothes from those shops because I didnt like any of them. They were not trendy in any way. On this instance I got no clothes. I felt inhuman, different. It confirmed for me that I was in the care system. I was just a number. Kids in ordinary homes don't have to use order books to buy clothes so why should I? Why was I seen as different? Things like this further messed up my head. I had enough to contend with without adding more to my fucked up head.

Being in care meant I had a certain amount of rights. One of these was to complain about anything that I was unhappy with. At my next review I asked if I could use cash to buy clothes. The social work manager at that time saw this as a formality. She knew instinctively that I was a sound kid and took a gamble of allowing me to have cash to buy clothes. The next day I was in town with a member of staff and one hundred pounds in real

Going Into Care

money. It was brilliant. I was trusted and treated as any other kid would be. I knew there were guidelines and budgets and all that. But surely these sort of things could be overcome instead of being so rigid? Maybe this was because the boss and his wife who were of the school of thought – deserving/undeserving poor. I knew his heart was in the right place, but his workings were slightly outdated.

A few months later the boss retired and was replaced by someone else. At our first meeting he gave me a firm handshake and a stern glance. He was the boss and he wanted me to know it. And I did know it!

During this time I had formed a relationship with a member of staff. She was really good and I felt I could talk to her. She was very honest and very open. I suppose in a way all of the staff were very nice. They seemed to care, but at times they seemed to get bogged down in the bureaucracy of 'the system'. I knew at times when they were making decisions that their hands were tied. They were responsible to the Officer-In-Charge. One distinct thing I remember about him was that he didn't take any shit from anyone. He was that type of guy!

I remember on one occasion I used to get bus tokens to get to school, which I felt was degrading, but that's a different story. Anyway, when I got my tokens for the day I used to walk part of the distance or even ask for more tokens as I was getting a different bus and route. At first this worked quite well and I managed to 'rip him off' about a pound at a time. With these extra tokens I would sell them to friends at school at a reduced rate. Possibly a twenty pence token for ten pence coin. I would use this money to buy fags or sweets. This system worked well for about two months.

My downfall was confiding in my younger brother who then began a similar system at his school. Unfortunately he got caught selling them to one of his friends. In turn, the headmaster phoned the home. When my younger brother got home he was confronted by Alex who went mad at him. He was shouting and screaming that his pocket money would be stopped for months. Among all this my brother let it slip that I had been doing it for months and nobody had said anything to me. I was caught. I was finally snared. The mature Mark was not the golden boy anymore.

Going Into Care

When I arrived home he was waiting for me. 'Hi Mark, had a good enterprising day have you?' He said sarcastically. I replied 'yeah it was alright'. 'Get in that office you little weasel' he roared at the height of his voice. Whilst in the office I opened up to the lies and deceit I had given to him for the past few months. My punishment was that I would lose two pounds off my pocket money which at the time was four pounds and ten pence. This sanction was to last for two weeks. He also told me that the trust I had earned was out the window and that it would have to be earned back.

While all this was going on, and I suppose while my development as a difficult, obnoxious. answering back, want my own way adolescent was coming along nicely, my younger brother was getting ever more unhappy. This was due to my father promising him new bikes, a new life and love. All the things my father was incapable of realistically offering. In my brother's eyes my father had reformed really making an effort to get him home. The social worker wanted this too as she felt that the care system would not benefit or do anything for my younger brother. He needed a family environment to further his development.

During this time we had a change of social worker. She was on the ball and didn't let the grass grow under her feet, Caroline was her name. I used to meet her once a week in a diner in town for a meal. If I wanted something all I had to do was ask. I didn't always get it, but I tried.

I had been in the home for nearly a year and was responding well. Words like independent living, moving on, were all floating around my personal space. One positive thing that happened was that I managed to get a seasonal job at a local fairground. I was earning £10 per day for eight hours. I began working on the waltzer, but after an accident I was put working with gambling machines and videos. I met lots of new friends. I was spreading my wings and getting out of the care environment. I had plenty of money and enjoyed the work. I worked the school holidays – full-time and 'skivved' school until the end of September so I could work until the end of the season. Something had to be sacrificed and school was not my priority.

Going Into Care

Although I 'skivved' school my attendance had improved by one hundred per cent. In my final year, which was the same year I got the seasonal job, I spent a lot of time and effort studying my 'o' levels. I finally passed four of them which was a major achievement for me.

With the money I earned at the carnival, I was saving up to by myself a new stereo, some clothes and a Vespa 50cc. Altogether I saved up six hundred and fifty pounds. I had worked hard for it. I bought all three. I had to wait a bit of time before I could ride my scooter as I was not sixteen for another six months. I waited in anticipation. I cleaned it everyday, sat on it hundreds of times and started the engine just to check the timing. It was all mine. I had something that I had bought with my money. My 'real' money. Also I was one of the 'Mods'. I had reached my dream of being the 'Ace'.

All of this maturity I was showing was adding up to me moving on. I was beginning to outlive the children's home. I was now sixteen.

At my review everyone heard how well I was getting on. I was praised for my efforts. I couldn't understand this because I was only doing what I felt was natural, for me. I was offered the opportunity to move to an independent living unit.

My social worker arranged a visit for me to meet the Officer-In-Charge. Our visit went really well. I felt really at ease with this guy. The unit was a huge place at first sight. It was set in its own grounds away from the community – or so I thought it was. At the time before I moved in, the home was split into three parts. One part of the house was still the children's home where about eight kids shared communal living. The other two parts of the house were split into semi-independent living on the ground floor and totally independent living on the floor above. I was going into the semi-independent living part. This was a bit like the children's home in the way that there were staff around to help you, but they did not do the cooking for you. That was done on your own. They were there to help or offer advice if you needed it.

I was all set to move in a few weeks time. The week after I was due to move, my brother went back home to my father who was now living with another woman and planning to get married. My brother was happy.

Going Into Care

My move to the unit was put on hold as there were massive problems within the home. The local community wanted rid of the home, closed down. What about the kids who are living there I thought? These young people were even more disturbed that the Slims of this world. All types of solvents were being sniffed, alcohol was being drunk and violence was a frequent occurrence. The staff worked so hard to try and contain these problems, but it was overspilling into the local community. The turning point was when a young person died of gas inhalation on his birthday . The residents went crazy, they could not handle this. This was too much. The staff also found it difficult to believe. The local residents had a field day. It was ammunition to get rid of the home. They came to us blazing their guns. How could anyone justify what had happened? The boss did! He was our driving force. He was behind the staff and worked in the kids best interests. He managed to keep it open but under certain conditions. Some of the residents had to go. A sacrifice had to be made.

After the death of Graham blew over, I moved in. The next few months that followed were sheer hell for me. The majority of the peer group were on solvents. None of them had moved out yet. I suppose the social work managers were biding their time. One final complaint from the community would be the point where things had to change.

It was difficult for me as I wanted to be part of the group. I had the choice, either to sniff with them, or face being beaten up while I slept. These were constant threats that not just me but everyone was faced with. You had to be with them not against them. I sniffed with them because it was the easy way out. We used to sniff in the grounds because they were wooded and very secluded. I only did this for a short time to make friends-that's all. This didn't work.

By this time they knew I was a Mod. Some of the residents were into punk music which did not mix with Mod music. By now I had my Vespa and had managed to park it in a shed out of the way.

One day I had been into town meeting my mates and had come home to pick up some records that I was lending to a mate. I parked my Vespa near the front of the house. Minutes later when I came out of the house it was on the floor. Someone had kicked it over and the mirrors had been smashed. That was it: I had had enough. I stormed into the pool room where all the residents were sat and 'asked who had kicked my bike over'. One of the young people stood up and 'asked what the fuck is he murmuring about?' My actions spoke larger than words. I hit him three times before he hit the floor. No-one else moved an inch. If they did I was ready for them. I asked if anyone else wanted to 'have a go'. There was no reply. I turned and walked out.

I was avoided for a few days until they all got their giros. They all came home early one evening to 'do me in'. They had all got hard because of the drink they had consumed. Four of them walked into the pool room where I was playing pool with a member of staff. They picked up cues and some snooker balls. The balls were thrown through the windows while cues were smashed against the pool table. I said 'that was shit because they had missed me'. This aggravated the situation, but I was holding my ground. This was as much my home as theirs. As the situation got worse I was ushered away from the incident very quickly by the staff. As we left a mini-riot took place. The pool room was wrecked. Forty windows were broken and several cars in the area were damaged. In the days that followed a higher management decision was made to move certain individuals out as soon as possible. A house meeting was called. All the residents and staff were present, and some social work managers. We discussed at length happenings over the past few weeks. Then it was crunch time! We were all asked if we wanted to make a go of the place. They wanted real answers, real commitments. They knew who didn't give a shit and who did. They did not want 'err, buts, or 'dunno'. They wanted 'yes'. They went through the whole group and eventually ended up with three yes's out of ten. That was Billy, Lisa and myself. We had committed ourselves to some very hard tasks – forging new relationships within the community, suggesting new ideas towards a better unit, what as young people we wanted as a service. It was going to be hard work.

In the next few days that followed all the 'no's' were moved on to supported lodgings or bed and breakfasts. We were in a process of change. In one way or another this was not really addressing the recurring issues in their lives, but merely passing on the buck. But saying that, there has

Going Into Care

to be a time when enough is enough. This time had passed long ago. The sixty thousand dollar question was has the system done them an injustice? What did these young people really want from the care system?, or were they using the system for their own gain? Did they want someone to love and care for them or someone who doesn't give a shit? Looking back I don't feel that people at the time didn't give a shit. A lot of work had been put into keeping these kids in care, but maybe this was one of the reasons they were so fucked up. Residential work is very hard work. To get it right is fundamentally impossible. In theory you can get it right. In practice, with individual personalities all giving different messages to kids, you end up with a 'mixed up' group. Something had definitely gone wrong somewhere. Was it their upbringing or lack of it? Or was it the care system? Who knows! After they had all moved out we began to see new faces emerging as new referrals came to look around. A few young people were formally admitted. One young person whom I built up a friendship was Ian. We got on extremely well and had a lot in common. We were the same age and wanted similar things in life – our own independence.

It was now 1985, and I was nearly seventeen. I was still working at the local fairground. I had sold my scooter and was now taking driving lessons. Christmas was just around the corner. I was still into music, but many of the groups I liked had split up. Groups like The Jam, Madness, The Specials, Purple Hearts, Squire and many others. I felt the Mod era that I was so much a part of slowly dwindling away. Scooters Inc had virtually disappeared, only to be replaced by Scooter boys and Northern Soul. I liked Northern Soul, but it wasn't like the Mod scene. It wasn't thrashy. It wasn't political. It was slow, romantic and tiresome. By this time I began to listen to groups like Simple Minds, Tears for Fears, U2, Big Country and lots of other groups around in the charts at the time. There was a lot of good music around.

We had a very busy year in the unitl. I had attended some local community meetings, organised sales of work and coffee mornings. The unit was beginning to work. Our initial aims had been met, but we still had lots of work to do.

Going Into Care

During this time I had a few job interviews. One I remember in particular was for a Y.T.S. welder / engineer. It must have been about November time. My job at the fair was only seasonal so I had finished for the summer. I went for the job and as I always did I presented as a mature, keen hard worker. The job was handed to me on a silver platter. I could start on the following Monday. I was over the moon. I could hardly contain myself in the chair in the guy's office. At the end of the interview the interviewer asked what my address was, as I had written down the unit's name. I told him it was an Independence Training Unit for young people. In his eyes I saw Children's Home and 'oh no here comes trouble'. I knew right away that I wasn't going to get the job after all. He then said 'give me a second until I check a starting date for you,' which he had already given me. He left the room and returned minutes later and said 'thank you for attending our interview. We will phone you about whether you have got the job or not and to give you a starting date'. I shook his hand and walked out disappointed.

When I got home the staff asked how I had got on and I said 'they would contact me soon'. I knew this was bullshit! On that day my life took a turn for the worse. I went out to a local D.I.Y. shop and bought some glue. I needed to escape from what I was feeling inside. Sniffing glue gave me that opportunity. I sniffed furiously for nearly five hours. By this time I was well out of my head, I was aggressive and very abusive. When challenged about sniffing I said 'fuck off and leave me alone'. I then went to my room to sleep it off. The next day I decided to open up and say why I had sniffed the day before. I was really close to my Officer-In-Charge. He was the only person I felt I could off load on to. Unfortunately he was not around that day. He was in meetings somewhere else. This fused me more. The more I thought about the interview the more depressed I became. I kept thinking to myself but I have done so well, worked so hard to be accepted, I have kept my side of the bargain, I have done very little that was wrong, I am a human being. But to the outside world I was a failure, a thief, a rouge, a bastard, a criminal, a child in care! That was my C.V. and I should accept that. I should live up to that expectation, that would then confirm it for people in the outside world, the real world. I lived in

73

Going Into Care

the inside world and was not going to be accepted elsewhere until I could prove I was worth it. I had tried this and failed. The staff had every confidence in me and were the only people who accepted me for what I was, not for what I should be.

With all these feelings running through my brain I again needed to escape. This was the easy way out. This was what the outside world wanted. So I did. I began to sniff regularly. Spent all my money on glue. I gradually slipped from my achievement perch to a crouched position on the ground. I was vulnerable and susceptible towards my addiction of substance abuse. The staff had seen dramatic changes in my personality, character and behaviour.

Another turning point for me was that I had contacted my younger brother, which in turn, meant some contact with my father. What was happening to me I wondered? I was regressing. Going backwards, and I couldn't stop it. I didn't want to go down that path, but I had to experience it. I had to find out what I really felt towards my father.

At first it was great. We went to the pub as father and son. We would both get drunk and go back to his house and fall asleep until it was time for me to go home.

Back at the home I would sniff glue. I was going in a backwards circle. I was following in my father's footsteps – something I had never wanted to do. For some odd reason something was innately driving me in that direction. It was only after a few weeks that I realised what was happening to me. I decided on that day and at that precise moment that I would not see my father anymore. He wasn't very happy but I just stopped contacting him. I needed time to think, not to drink.

While this was going on I had been to another job interview with the Water Board. I was due to start on the Monday. This job I did get. Unfortunately, I was still sniffing glue. I had managed to web Ian and another lad Simon into my hallucination sessions.

It was now approaching the Christmas of 1985 I remember it distinctively because it snowed for about two weeks over Christmas and New Year. It was also very cold. I had been working for a few weeks and was enjoying the work. I wasn't looking forward to Christmas at all. It was a time that families spent together. Sharing and caring, and all that shit! What a fucking hypocrisy. Be nice to each other because its fucking Christmas. Here's some toys for the home and have a nice Christmas. Just wait until after Christmas and we'll treat you like shit again. What a fucking society!!

Anyway, I finished work on the twenty-third of December. I headed straight to our local B & Q and bought four litres of Evo-Stik. This would last me a few days at least. When I got home I found to my surprise that Ian had also got some glue from work. We were going to have a party. We sniffed that evening, out in the grounds, in the snow.

We sniffed all day and evening of Christmas Eve. I remembered just before midnight I was buzzing away into the sky when I suddenly saw a light in the distance. I nudged Ian who was next to me and said 'hey what is that?' in a slurred voice. Ian replied by saying 'its Santa'. As I buzzed more he came closer until his sleigh was hovering right above our heads. A magical ladder appeared next to me and Santa came down it. He said 'Hello Mark have you been a good boy?' I replied in a truthful voice 'yes Santa I have'. He then handed me a present and said 'not to open it until he had left'. I put the present on the floor and watched Santa deliver presents to our home. When he finished he waved and disappeared. This all lasted about ten minutes. I went to pick up my present but it had gone. I was gutted. Something else had been taken from me. Just like my mother had been. I hated this life. Things were given, but more than often taken away.

I woke on Christmas morning to find a few presents outside my bedroom door. The staff were singing merrily and preparing a right good Christmas feast. We had a really good day. Just like the one's I used to have. We didn't sniff that day but we did the day after. Altogether we sniffed about six litres of glue in three days. This was not doing our body or brain any good. The festive period and into the New Year was the worst time for everyone. While normal families – especially with mum and dad there – were all loving and caring. We did not have that. We had the material Christmas, but not the emotional one that we all really wanted. Saying that, we had a really good Christmas and New Year. We decided

Going Into Care

to get rather drunk. The staff were also very good and shared in the day. If it wasn't for the staff it would have been shitty.

Chapter Twelve

STIGMA

After Christmas and New Year it was back to work. Back to real life. Reality faced us again. Non-acceptance slapped us in the face. Nothing had changed. Perhaps we had changed. Perhaps the drugs had made us change. This was confirmed for me when an incident occurred at a bus stop from which I used to catch the bus to work.

As usual I caught the bus at 7.20am to get me to work before 8am. On this particular day it was raining heavily. I was soaked to death before I even got to the bus stop. There was no one else at the bus stop when I arrived there. A few minutes later two women and a man arrived at the bus stop. At first they were talking amongst themselves. Then I suddenly felt their eyes in the back of my head. Then the knife was in my back. I am speaking metaphorically here of course. I heard one say 'he's one from that place, that home'. I turned and looked at them but my fate was sealed. They had judged me before I even opened my mouth. I had said nothing and had not offended them in any way. I offended them because of my presence. I said nothing as I knew that community relations were not very good at that moment in time. After that I heard them laugh and snigger. I was not a happy person. Minutes later the bus arrived. As I walked to get on the bus I was nudged out of the way by the man who then said 'women first, have you no manners?' I could hardly contain myself. My eyes filled up and my adrenaline was pumping at one hundred miles a second around my body. I got on the bus and went upstairs to sit at the back. I punched the back of the seat, in front of me, until I was bleeding. This saved me from killing that guy. I'll tell you now it was one of the hardest things I had to ever do and that was to restrain myself.

STIGMA

No wonder all the other kids including myself in care had chips on our shoulders. In a way I could not stop or prevent the chip from growing ever worse, primarily because it was constituted from and directed by other people. This was affecting my self-image, self-esteem and my confidence, which in turn added to my anger and frustration. It filled that bottle a little bit more inside me every time something like this happened. By this time the bottle was ready to explode.

The ironic thing about our situation, or any care home for that matter, was that regardless of where it was people didn't want it in their community. Not on our front door please! was the attitude. If this was the case then where were we to live? In a prison possibly! Behind bars and under control. We were not to be treated as humans and not to be given the opportunity to make mistakes and also to learn from them like everyone else.

The city had become very affluent because of the oil business. It had prospered for the past ten years or so. In a sense this was related to the fucked up attitude around. There was a huge gap between those who had nothing and those who had money coming out of their ears. Nobody could give a toss about people who were in need of support. As long as I am alright then that's enough for me was the attitude. The city's success had proved to be its downfall. I could not comprehend that so much wealth could cause so much grief.

The area that the unit was situated in was a predominantly middle to upper class area. A lot of the residents had done rather well out of the oil industry. They seemed to be very community orientated, helping each other out in difficult times. Money was never a issue for the local community. They seemed on the face of things to be a caring community, or so they aspired to be when they went to church and had coffee with the vicar afterwards. But back at their homes they were planning to make our lives as difficult as possible. Devious and degrading tactics were used to get us out of their community. It was bad enough being rejected by parents and the education system, to mention but a few. We had now been rejected by the community.

In the unit I was preparing myself for independence. I was buying and cooking my own food. I was doing my own laundry. I was keeping my room tidy and myself hygienically clean. The staff were around to offer support and advice twenty-four hours a day. They were really an understanding and caring bunch. I used to sit for hours talking to staff about my background. I found this therapeutic. It allowed me to express myself without being judged. I felt I fitted in. The staff did understand what it was like to be in care.

By this stage, and my mature outlook on life, the staff saw me a valuable resource to have around the unit. They knew I had an important position in the peer group. I was the influencing factor in the unit. I contolled the peer group. I had them in my hands. I knew I had this power and the understanding of how to use it. I was one of the most mature in the group. In a way this prompted the staff to encourage me to chat to and show around young people who might be coming to stay at the unit in the near future. After I had done this I would give my opinion as to whether I thought that particular young person was suitable or not. This was helpful for staff, although it was not a determining factor in whether a person came or not. I also began to take an interest in other residents. When they were on downers I used to chat to them for hours on end, listening to their horrific stories of abuse and their childhoods. I even took one or two of them for a few tins at the local off-licence. In most cases this worked really well because some of the residents would open up.

Anyway, three months later I was still sniffing glue. On this particular evening, sometime at the beginning of spring, Ian, Simon and myself were in the grounds sniffing. Ian and Simon were heavily into buzzing 'Lord of The Rings' which they were both reading. I concentrated my energies into a song written by Echo and the Bunnymen – The Cutter. I used to listen to it before we went sniffing. This enhanced my chances of buzzing certain things.

We were all walking along an old path when Simon who was wearing a bright yellow boiler suit to save his clothes getting covered in glue, suddenly shouted 'a Black Rider hide'. We all dived to the ground for cover. Simon decided to go and fight him. Simon was hallucinating all of this of course. The figure he saw was a hallucinationary figure. Ian and I stood and watched. Simon ventured off to a battlefield. A little later Simon returned to join us saying he had fended him off and eventually killed him. We walked on a bit further to a big oak tree. We were all walking in the same direction. Suddenly Simon looked behind us and said 'don't move lads, there's a fucking huge lion behind us'. At that moment Ian and I looked behind to see nothing. As we did this Simon was off running like a madman. All I saw was this banana on legs. Ian and I could do nothing for laughing.

Every night we sniffed was different. On several occasions I became very violent and punched one of my mates in the face, amongst others. On this occasion I was sniffing beside a tree which I used to always get a good buzz off. Shortly afterwards I was joined by Ian and Simon. We all sniffed together. A few minutes later I noticed that Ian and Simon were buzzing the opposite way from me. I got very paranoid and thought they had done this intentionally to take the piss out of me. To top it all I heard them laughing. Again I thought it was aimed at me. I turned and stood in front of Simon and Ian. I said 'what's so funny, are you taking the piss?' Ian and Simon looked in amazement at me. I took this the wrong way as well. I punched Simon in the face several times. He fell to the ground. As I questioned Ian, Simon made a hectic dash for his life. He went into the home to sort out his head. I had no direct control over these actions. They just happened.

On one other occasion when I was sniffing with one of the other kids, Lewis, I remember walking down the pavement of a main road sniffing glue. As I was walking down the road it turned into liquorice and Lewis thought he was spiderman. I, on the other hand walked into the middle of the road which I thought was liquorice. I could see no cars. All I could see was liquorice allsorts on the liquorice. I thought it was great. Little did I know that the liquorice allsorts were cars. Luckily I did not get run over. I only got off the road when I saw a beckoning allsort on the fence that Lewis was climbing. When I got to the other side the 'buzz' wore off slightly. I started sniffing again and this time a river suddenly replaced the road. This time I had to swim across. I put my feet in the water and began to make the actions of swimming across the road. Again the cars came to a halt. Their was chaos on the road. I only realised what I had been doing after I came out of the 'buzz'. By this time it might have been to· late. I had been very lucky.

I only stopped sniffing, which was very difficult, when it suddenly dawned on me what I was doing. I was following in the footsteps of my older brother who had a sniffing problem during his teen's.

I have very vivid memories of my brother's problem. I was in a shopping centre with my father. This was where we lived a few years before. I think I must have been about twelve years old at the time. We came out of the centre to see a young man on the floor being sick. A glue bag was next to him. As we walked by he looked up. It was my brother. My father grabbed him by the scruff of his neck and dragged him back to my grandmother's. He was sat down, shouted at and slapped across the head several times. My brother was so out of it that he just laughed in my father's face.

When this memory came back I stopped sniffing. I could not face living in my brother's shadow. I knew I had been but now I consciously knew I had to do something about it. I stopped within a few weeks. It was not easy, but I did it.

This posed another problem for me. I was the one who in a sense started the glue business with Ian and Simon. It was my responsibility to get them off it. With Simon it was easy because he had had enough with the fight we had and all that. Ian on the other hand was addicted and enjoyed sniffing too much.

Apart from Ian there was another young kid, Lewis, whom I had sniffed with before. He used to sniff all the time. He wasn't in work so he had more time. I began to spend a lot of time talking to him about why he was sniffing glue. Also why he was in care and what pissed him off? We got on really well. Several times I managed to get him off solvents, but later found he had broken into somewhere to earn some cash for drink. In most cases he got caught by the police. You can't always win. He ended up doing a long stretch. He spent a lot of time inside. A few years later I heard that he had committed suicide while serving a sentence in a Young Offenders institution. What a waste of a life.

I was now beginning to get my head together. I began to take driving lessons after my seventeenth birthday. I took six lessons and passed. I had done something successful again.

Independence was getting ever so close. By now I should have been socially conditioned to live in the real world. Very soon I would have a tenancy for a flat, responsibilities and lots of other things I should conform to. I was now an adult and expected to behave like one. But there was one very important ingredient that I had not tasted and that was loneliness. Being in care provided me with a safe environment, people to talk to, people around all of the time. I was always around people. I had been institutionalised.

In the few weeks that followed, I filled in application forms for numerous Housing Associations and registered with the local council office. I was offered the opportunity of viewing a property. Which I did. Two weeks later I moved in. It was a planned move and I felt confident about moving. I had saved some money and also received a leaving care grant which would help to buy furniture, etc. I had come a long way and felt I had achieved something. I had not done it all myself. All the staff that I have known knew what my capabilities were. At times they pushed me to my limit. Other times I pulled back to the solitude of my own space – my bedroom. At other times I became abusive, unco-operative and stubborn. I turned to solvents. I even cut myself intentionally quite often. My self destruction button was nearly pushed several times, but something always held me back. That little something I believe was my mother. I knew not to go into the funeral rest rooms that time, I knew not to top myself when things got bad, but most important of all is that my mother was a strong person. She had the capacity to carry on, whatever stood in her way. She was now guiding me and I was comfortable in following her. I remember many years ago just after my mum died, my grandmother on my mum's side, said to me 'your mum will be watching whatever you do, she is caring for you and will forever love you'. I lived by this, and many times found myself crying myself to sleep with these thoughts

STIGMA

In a sense I was now alone just as when I was left outside the school, when my father didn't want me, when I was left on the pavement. But it was different. I controlled the decisions about my life, not the system anymore or my father. It was a positive move for me.

Chapter Thirteen
Digging my own grave

I was now living in my own flat. I was totally independent. I had achieved my goal. All the hard work of listening to the staff over the years had paid off. But I must admit it had not been easy. I enjoyed living on my own to begin with. Luckily for me I was in full-time employment and only had to fill my evenings. If I had been out of work it might have proved more difficult.

I kept in contact with my social worker, residential staff and also Ian with whom I had formed a really good relationship.

I suppose the first few months were a test for me. They did prove quite difficult at times. This was because at first I would have the odd sniff of glue in the flat. I remember sniffing mostly at night. I would stick on a Madness album and 'buzz' right through it, only to reach the rainbow at Nightboat To Cairo. I am sure the neighbour's could smell it, but they said nothing.

On an other occasion I had a magic mushroom party. There were about six of us in the flat preparing mushroom tea. We put the mushrooms into a tea pot and brewed them until the LSD was extracted and in the tea. We then drank the foul liquid as quickly as possible. After that we just waited for the 'buzz'. Twenty minutes later nothing had happened. We all decided to go for a walk to the local chippy. When we were inside ordering our 'suppers' – the word we use to describe a meal from a chippy – I began to feel very funny. I tried to order a supper, but looked at the guy serving me and burst out laughing. At first he thought I was mad. Everytime I tried to speak or look at the guy I burst out laughing. Very soon later everyone was experiencing the same. The guy on the other hand took offence to our fits of laughter. We eventually got thrown out

Digging my own grave

of the chippy. Our walk back to my house was unbelievable. Everytime I moved there was a ripple behind me of about fifty of me. It was like a long queue of me waiting at a bus stop. I was finding it very difficult to walk or even think for that matter. When we did get back to the house we all sat in the dark hallucinating for about six hours until it started wearing off. The worst thing is when the 'buzz' begins to wear off. The come down is foul. Its disgusting. Its draining to the body. It took me about two days to recover from the after affects.

My eldest brother Steven, even visited on one occasion. Only because his girlfriend lived and worked locally. But something was not right. I was getting into a boring routine. Getting up for work. Doing some shopping or laundry. Going to bed. Get up for work. I was in a rutt that I didn't like. I didn't want this now. Not yet anyway! I didn't know what I wanted. I soon found out.

I tried to make the best of it. I had a flat, television, video, stereo, furniture, a good job and also the use of the works van and on top of all that I had a second-hand car. What else could anyone my age want? I had my own independence, and I was beginning to hate it. One escape for me was to buy some beer or visit the local pub. This soon became a habit. I began drinking regularly. Very soon I was living in the footsteps of my father. Beer was different from drugs. It was more acceptable and tolerated in moderation. I had to break this habit as well.

So far the realities of life had slapped me from both sides. On one side I had my glue sniffing problem. Like my brother had. Whilst on the other side I had drink; my father's addiction. Walking in their footsteps was painful enough as it was. Where did my footsteps begin? When would my life become my own and not a shadow of my father's or brother's? Something needed to be done. I needed a way out.

My life only changed when I was introduced to a new staff member at work. She was a Kiwi and was on a working holiday – travelling around the world. I spent endless hours chatting to her about places she had visited – India, China, Thailand, Australia, Europe, Egypt. Her plans for the future were to go America and Canada. I couldn't get enough. I wanted a fix of the travelling bug. I really needed to go and soon. All I needed was

Digging my own grave

about five hundred pounds, a return flight, some of my meagre belongings, oh and most importantly a 'Work your way around the World' guide. This book was to prove a 'Bible' for me. This was my first footstep. This was the direction I needed. This was my way out. It offered me another chance to change my life. Do something I really wanted to do.

In about a month I had saved three hundred pounds. I had planned on selling the furniture in my flat to my mate Ian for three hundred quid. This would give me six hundred altogether. All I needed now was to pluck up the courage to go and book a flight. I had planned to do this a week before I intended leaving. This would give me time to give notice to my employer, to the Housing Association who had given me the tenancy, and to sort out outstanding bills, etc. I also had the hard job of departing from my friends, Ian especially.

So on the 27th of March 1987 I went into the travel agent with a hundred pounds of my money and asked 'where can I go for a hundred pounds'. The guy behind the counter replied 'Greece is quite good this time of the year and it is reasonably cheap for flights'. Within ten minutes I was signed, sealed and ready for departure. I came out of the shop full of excitement and with challenge written in my eyes. I was leaving in a week. I was flying to Athens. I told my employer and all the relevant people. When I told Ian he could not believe it. He thought I was mad. Giving up all that I had. I said 'But I can have this when I get back. I have plenty of time. I have my whole life ahead of me'.

In the week that followed I had a leaving party to which staff and residents from the unit were invited. I didn't have the balls to tell them I was leaving the country. I was the about to tell the biggest lie of my life. I told everyone I was going to a drama school in Glasgow. I knew of one and used its name and address, little to my knowledge so did my Officer-In-Charge. He knew something was fishy but did not say. I had also told Ian I was leaving on the Friday but actually left the day before, the Thursday. I really could not face saying goodbye to anyone. I opted for the easy cop out.

I suppose one of the other reasons why I told the lie was because, initially, Chae – short for Charlie – was going with me. He also lived in the

Digging my own grave

unit. He was on probation for a few outstanding offences. If people found out we were going they might have put a stop to our plans. Looking back now and travelling on my own I feel better that Chae lost his job when he did. Not due to me of course, but to his laziness and being continually late for work.

The night before I was due to leave I packed very little. Some clothes, trainers and some photo's of my mum. Everything else I had, personal things that I wanted to keep, I put in a suitcase and wrote on it that I wanted it kept in storage, until my return. I threw out loads of things. I was getting rid of all my bad baggage. As I did so I seemed to feel better. It was having a psychological effect on me. The old family footsteps began to disappear. My own had appeared. I was looking forward to the prospect of getting away. To start again. To have no-one giving me hassle. No family problems to grind me down. I was accountable to myself.

Chapter Fourteen

The seed is sown

As I left my flat on that Thursday I felt good. I stood at the door until the taxi driver was fed up honking his horn. I pulled the door closed and put the key through the letter box. There was no turning back now. I picked up my rucksack and small haversack and got in the taxi. As we drove down the street I looked over my shoulder, a huge smile erupted on my face. I could not contain myself. I must have bored the driver to death about me going on a working holiday. I couldn't get my words out quick enough. He drove me to the station where I boarded a train to London. This was the first leg of my journey. The train journey took eight hours. I spent most of the journey reading my Work your way around the World. I had read it about twenty times before I even got to London.

I arrived in London at 6.40am. I had a breakfast in the station cafe'. Then I got onto the tube and headed for Heathrow Airport. I was due to check-in at 9.30am. I booked in as planned and spent an hour looking around the duty free shops.

My plane left as scheduled. Flying was a first for me. I did not know what to expect. As we pulled out onto the runway my heart was beating twice as fast. I was shitting myself. My eyes were fixed at the runway outside. I didn't even have second thoughts about going. My hands were tightly gripping the arms of the seat in front of me. As we took off my face said it all. I was as happy as a pig in muck.

It took just over four hours to fly to Athens. In that time I made the terrible mistake of accepting loads of free in-flight drinks. I was rather pissed when we landed. As I got off the plane the heat slapped me right in the face. It was 28°C. In other words really hot.

The seed is sown

My next plan of action was to get a bus or taxi into the city because I had a few addresses of hostels out of my 'Bible' that I could stay in as a starting point. I got through customs and headed for the first taxi I saw. I said to the taxi driver in a very broad Scottish accent 'take me tae the city mate'. At this he looked at me in utter amazement and incomprehension. He was probably thinking I had just landed from outer space. I knew then that I would have to curb my Scottish tongue. I would have to speak plainer English and lose the dialect right away.

I arrived in a city which I knew nothing of. I didn't know the language. The food I had never experienced before. Most of the food I had never heard off, and most depressing of all, they didn't have any McEwans Export. Fortunately this was not the end of the world and I soon got used to the change in life style.

The trip from the airport to the city took about fifteen minutes. While in the taxi I had given the driver the address of a hostel I wanted to stay in. As we neared the city I could see the big office buildings and lots of houses. They were different from the city life I was used to. They looked like shacks built out of white plaster. While going through the city centre the taxi driver was showing me the sights. I didn't want the sights yet. As he was driving there meter was going faster and I knew I was going to get 'ripped off'. After he had pointed out Gateway to Poseidon, the museum and The Tomb of The Unknown Soldier, I decided enough was enough. Just as he announced we were approaching the Acropolis I shouted 'at the height of my voice stop the car now Jimmy'. With that he said 'no problem'. As I later found out this saying is the fundamentals of all Greek philosophy. They all say it in response to anything good or bad. When he didn't stop the taxi I said 'to him in an angry voice if you don't stop this fucking car now I'll rip your head off and shit down your neck'. With that he stopped the car. I got out. Got my rucksack from the boot of the car and asked how much I was owe him. He said 'five thousand Drachma,' which at the time was equivalent to about twenty five quid. There was no way I was paying that. I threw him two thousand Drachma and told him to 'piss off'. I walked about five hundred yards with the taxi driver yelling 'Mafioso' after me. On the same side of the road was a pension – the name

The seed is sown

for a small hotel. In about five minutes I was booked in and the whole incident with the taxi driver was a past experience. I had a shower and went for some food and an ice cold beer. I needed to have a gander at my new environment and to suss-out my new territory. Within an hour I had met a few of the travellers who were living in the hostel. We went out on the piss, shared experiences of where everyone had travelled, and exchanged addresses of good places to eat, work and play. I later found out that the taxi drivers were always ripping travellers off. I was told to sort out a price before even getting into a taxi, one of the best pieces of advice I was ever to encounter.

After about a week of living the high life I decided to try and find some work. One fellow traveller I had met was from Czechoslovakia. He had fled from there as he was wanted for national service. He also was an outspoken citizen. This in Czechoslovakia was strictly forbidden. He had escaped overland through Yugoslavia: all by foot. He had no money and had been in Athens for nearly a year. As he was saving, he had two jobs, so that he could live away as long as possible. Through the day he worked in a boat yard, whilst at night he worked as a kitchen porter in a Greek restaurant in the Plaka – the area of Athens where everything happens, nightlife, food, beer, etc. He said a guy he knew had just left his job at the boatyard. and that if I was interested to go with him the next morning. So I did. I started the job of preparing the boats for spraying and refurbishment the next day. The job was about a ten minute bus ride from the city to a area called Glyfada. At first I would travel everyday to work but soon got fed up with it. My boss offered me the use of a small caravan – a two berth for me to live in for as long as I wanted to. I was soon living at the boatyard. I still kept in contact with the guys I had met in Athens – Calvin, the Czech and Graham. I really enjoyed the work at the boatyard. The hardest bit of the working day at the boatyard was Siesta. From about twelve-noon until about one-thirty everyone would go to sleep. At first I thought this was great until it came to half past one and I had to go back to work. I could not be arsed. I was absolutely shattered. I took me the month I was there to get used to it and by that time I was ready to move on. I managed to live on my earnings and to save some money for travelling expenses to

The seed is sown

the next place. I didn't dig into my savings. I had spent about a month in Athens and was now planning my next move.

Calvin, one of the first guys I had met was on his way to Turkey. I, on the other hand, planned to go to a small fruit picking village called Nafplion. It is north of Athens on the Peloponneses. Before leaving Athens I had visited all the sights, museums, eaten the food and had sampled plenty of the beer and Ouzo.

I left for the small village of Nafplion. I stayed in the local youth hostel and soon found my feet. The way to get work in this village was to turn up at about five in the morning and wait for work to turn up. First come first served was the motto. I managed to gain some work picking fruit for a small farmer.

On my days off I would lie about the beach with other travellers I had met. One day I managed to fall asleep on the beach only to be wakened by the sizzling of third degree burns on my back. I could hardly walk and spent a few days under a warm shower.

About a week later I met up with Calvin, the guy I had met in Athens. Calvin was South African and had been travelling for many years. A few days later we met another South African, called Rob. The three of us shared a room and worked for the same farmer. It was great. The room we rented for about £2 per night each had a shared kitchen and toilet. The shower was in the toilet and directly above the toilet bowl. This was to save you having to clean the toilet. It wasn't that hygienic I can tell you. We complained about this and also the price of the room. It was too expensive. We haggled a price of £1.25 per night with the landlady.

During my stay in that rented room I met some interesting characters. There was one guy who had been to Oxford and had degree's as long as his arm, but loved living on the breadline. He had about £20 to his name and no intention of going home. He loved that life. I met another guy who had escaped from Czechoslovakia. He had no money except what he had earned from working that day. He worked in a restaurant as a chef but was wanted by the Greek police in Athens for assault – which he said the Greeks had set him up with. His life story was quite amazing. He would

The seed is sown

hide in the cellar out of fear of being arrested and deported home to Czechoslovakia.

Calvin, Rob and myself became very lucky and managed to get some work from two farmers. Our job was to travel around with them on a tractor pulling an old wheat husker. We would travel to small villages in the mountains and husk their wheat for them. This involved putting wheat into the top of the machine, which would then shake and cut the wheat, which in turn, would produce seeds at one side and bales of hay at the other. It was really hard work. We started at dawn and finished at dusk. We got paid £15 per day and our food was thrown in for free. Our accommodation was around a small fire under the stars. Quite tranquil really. At meal times we ate a pig off the skewer. It was great. Beer was also aplenty. We did this for three weeks but by then we had had enough. So we went back to the small village of Nafplion where we relaxed on the beach and drank plenty of beer.

Soon after this I decided it was time to move on again. I parted present company – which for me was hard because I had built up good relationships with Calvin and Rob.

This time I headed for the islands. I didn't intend to work but instead only to play. I spent the next two months island hopping. I went to Ios, Santorini, Paxos, Mycanos, Rhodes, Corfu, Crete, Pavos and Cyprus.

I planned to meet up with Calvin in Crete, which we did, but unfortunately never saw Rob again.

Calvin and myself decided to board a boat and head towards Israel, hopefully to work on a Kibbutz. We spent three days on a boat and paid the minimum fare third class deck standard. In other words you slept on the deck. It was a great journey, no bad weather or anything. The only bad thing about deck class was that if the sea got a little choppy the swimming pool would overspill and the water would flow all over the deck. We managed to pick a good spot and only got splashed a few times. Other people were not so lucky.

Chapter Fifteen

The Holy Land

On arrival in Israel, at the port of Haifa, we headed for Tel-Aviv where we met up with a girl from Scotland. She was heading to a small Kibbutz outside Tel-Aviv which she had previously worked on. She told us that instead of going to the Kibbutz registration office we should go straight to a Kibbutz and ask for work. She also gave us the address of one about a mile from where she was going.

So we went. Lucky for us they had spaces for volunteers. We were shown to a room that we would have to share. We were given a tour of the Kibbutz – food hall, shops, swimming pool, cinema, gym, weights room and most importantly the bar. It was great. It had everything. We needed no money. Our food and lodgings were free.

The next day I was asked where I wanted to work and I said in the kitchen. Apparently I was given the best job on the Kibbutz. I started at 6am and finished at 11am, being given cakes, fruit, biscuits, meat; everything I needed. All I had to do was to cook vegetables, soup and make soft drinks. The snag was that it was for fifteen hundred people.

My first day consisted of revolutionising the taste of vegetables. I was told to put a cup of cinnamon and five cups of salt into a big vat of carrots. I got them mixed up and did the opposite. For the first time ever all the carrots had been eaten. Usually some would be thrown out, but this time people wanted more. Compliments were given to the chef Ezra and Abraham. They had no idea what had gone on. They came to me later that evening and asked what I had done. When I told them they asked me to continue making the carrots that way. I believe they a are still doing it now!

The Holy Land

This was the start of a great working experience. I spent the next three months getting pissed, getting suntanned, meeting new friends and working hard.

During my stay on the Kibbutz I changed job several times working, for example, in the kids crèche. It was very hard work as I did not know the lingo. I soon picked up the basics. I really enjoyed the work. This was when I realised that I enjoyed working with kids.

Kibbutz life for kids is very different from our way of bringing kids up in the U.K. The kids stay at the crèche all week and only go home at weekends, the Kibbuztinizm believing that children learn better at school and that parents are secondary figures. The love, caring and the sharing atmosphere is always there, but school is a vital part of it.

My next job was in a laundrette where I was ironing clothes for about two thousand people. I have never seen so many shirts and undies in all my life!

On the Kibbutz we also managed to get some time off to travel to Jerusalem, Tel-Aviv, Masada, The Dead Sea, The Sea of Galilee, Bethlehem, The Jordan Heights and Eilat. When I say we, I mean Calvin and a friend called Dave who arrived a few weeks after us. We had all become very close. It was as though we had known each other for years.

The three of us shared the same room. And our lives too. We were a great bunch. A friendship was formed. We were a bunch of practical jokers really. We were the life and soul of all the parties on the kibbutz. We organised barbecues and parties by the pool. I remember on one occasion it was my someone's twenty-first birthday party. He had been given a bottle of Pernod which he absolutely hated, so he gave it to me. I drank it in about an hour. I was totally legless. The wall in the disco was holding me up. I had to be carried home at an obscene hour as I had fallen asleep in the bushes. As I put my head onto the pillow the room began to spin at a hundred miles an hour. My stomach began to erupt. Sickness was on its way up, full steam ahead! I dashed for the toilet but, as always didn't make it. I missed the toilet by about three feet. This may seem a good miss but I'll tell you three feet is not bad when you're pissed out of your head.

The Holy Land

For the next three days all I could smell was Pernod. So could everyone else. The toilet never lost that odour as long as I was there.

As always all good things came to an end. A day of departure for one of us was just around the corner. Dave was the first to leave. He was returning to London his home ground. His leaving had a profound effect on me. I was devastated. I remember hugging him and watching him disappear into the distance. Then my emotions took over. I stood crying for about ten minutes. Calvin was there too. He had become immune to breaking down when friendships had to be broken. His travelling had made him hard in this respect. He had been through this ritual loads of times. He reassured me by saying that we should keep in contact with him.

About a week later I planned to leave the Kibbutz to travel to Sinai and then on to Egypt. Calvin was travelling to Cyprus and to Turkey again. I was going to be on my own again.

We both departed. It was the usual breakdown for me. For Calvin it was 'pull yourself together man,' in a jocular fashion. I could for the first time see a sparkle of a tear in his eyes. Maybe he wasn't so immune after all.

I had a few things I needed to do for myself. This had stemmed from my upbringing as a catholic. I went to Jerusalem and visited all the places that Jesus was supposed to have been – Golgotha, The Garden of Gethsemane, the Mount of Olives, his walk through the old city and the tomb where he was laid to rest. I tried for a few days to reconcile my feelings towards God and my religion. I found it ever more confusing when I found that there was so much controversy around where he was crucified, laid to rest, etc. On one side you have Christians arguing it was in their quarter. You have the Arab quarter arguing it was in theirs. What the fuck is going on? Who could I go to for advice? I went to the Christian quarter and got one story whilst in the Arab or Jewish quarter I got another. I tried within myself, but confusion clouded me. All of this stuff was not for me. I wanted real answers. I was not given them. In a sense I was forced to believe in something I could not. I left the city happier believing in myself, rather than several different messages.

The Holy Land

I travelled to Tel-Aviv where I met up with a guy called Scottie and a group of Kibbutz volunteers who were making the same trip. I later found out that Scottie had worked on the same Kibbutz as the girl from Scotland, who had given us the address of the Kibbutz I lived on. He knew her well. Its a small world I'll tell you!

I only spent the one night in Tel-Aviv because I had visited it previously. We left early the next morning. The coach trip to Cairo would take eight hours. We drove through the Gaza Strip clutching to the floor of the bus while bullets flew over our heads. What in the name of heaven was I doing? This was unbelievable.

We arrived in Cairo about eight hours later and were shown to our hotel, later going on for something to eat. You have to buy a package when you go to Egypt. This includes hotel, travel and breakfast. Our duration in Cairo was about a week.

I could not believe how cheap it was. Kebab's and hamburgers were 15p. A three course meal was £1.00. It was that cheap that one evening whilst asleep in the room I shared with Scottie I was wakened by my own voice and Scottie laughing his head off. When I asked what was funny Scottie said that I was continually saying my sleep 'its cheap, its bloody cheap'. A true Scotsman perhaps. And I loved every moment of it.

Whilst in Egypt we managed to get 'ripped off'. We paid 10p or 20p more than we should have for certain things. You have to remember we were on a tight budget. Well that's my excuse! I can't vouch for Scottie. We went to the pyramids at Giza, the famous Cairo museum, Saqquara, Luzor, Aswan, Abu Simbell, Lake Nasser. We also took a Faluka boat trip up the Nile, visited the Valley of the Kings and returned through Sinai stopping at a place that is rather like heaven if there is one, called Dahab.

On our way to Dahab we climbed Mount Sinai where Moses supposedly received the ten commandments. By now I was looking at religion, the Bible and Jesus, and all, that as a story. We spent the night there and froze our bollocks off. It was one of the longest nights of my life. There is a guy up there who will live there for the rest of his life. He will eventually be replaced by someone else when he passes away.

The Holy Land

I spent a week in Dahab. Which is known for its drug trade. The police are the only safe bet to buy it from but you do pay three or four US dollars more than you should for a 1lb of good black. Dahab is like paradise; you sleep in cane huts and eat outside on the Palm beach. There is no alcohol so all you can do is smoke three foot pipes all day. I spent a week among the stars, living on a different planet. Soon all this became a bit boring. Being spaced out all the time is seriously bad for you. I met some people who had been there for years living on dope. They were so fucked up. They knew so little of reality. After reality began to slip from me, I decided to move on, back to Eilat. Scottie was still with me. He decided enough was enough.

I had also bought some souvenirs in Dahab. One was a small pipe I had used several times for dope. I had scrapped it clean of any resin. Well, I thought I had. We knew that the Israelis were really tight on security, especially coming through from an Arab country. They saw my pipe and took it away to have it examined. Shortly after, I was being examined. I was asked a million questions, and then given a full body search by a women guard. She must have been about twenty and was beautiful. She stuck her finger right up my arse. I bet she loved it. I nearly asked her for a date as I was cleared to leave, but thought I had better not. She would probably have shot me through the head. Scottie was also searched, but not as thorough as I.

Chapter Sixteen

To be someone was a wonderful thing

I was now in Eilat looking for work. I went around all the hotel bars, restaurants and still could not find work. Scottie and myself had resorted to sleeping in a school playground, primarily because it cost us nothing. It saved us ten shequels a night, which was about four quid. We did this for a few days then my luck took a change for the better.

I was getting rather drunk one evening when I met a fellow Scotsman in a bar. As we continued to get drunk he offered me a job as an extra in Rambo III which was being filmed just outside Eilat. At first I thought it was a wind up. I thought he was a crazy Scotsman. Before we left he wrote down the name of a hotel where I could meet him the next morning at 5am. I left thinking what a piss head, but curiosity killed the cat. I woke with a blinding headache the next morning in the school playground and stumbled towards this hotel. At my arrival there were loads of people there. I was guided onto the bus after I gave them my name, which was ticked off. Away we went to some unknown oblivion. An hour and half later I was woken and asked to follow everyone else. There were about one hundred and fifty of us. We all had breakfast and then were carted off to some huge tents where we picked up a Russian commando uniform and exchanged our passports for an AK47 sub-machine gun. I got dressed, and in my drunken daze still could not comprehend what was going on. I asked Scottie who was there as well to pinch me to waken me up.

After I got dressed I was asked to stand in line with everyone else. A few minutes later a producer or somebody shouted 'Good morning'. It was still the middle of the night I thought. We all replied with sleepy murmurs 'Good morning'. He then said 'Mr Stallone will be arriving in a few minutes and when he does he will walk between everyone and will

To be someone was a wonderful thing

pick people he wants to work closely with him. He will tap you on the shoulder. If he does, come and stand at the side of me. Alright!' I still thought I was dreaming. Minutes later there was a cavalcade of four-wheel jeeps emerging through a dust storm. Sylvester Stallone was in front of me within minutes, surrounded by armed bodyguards. It was true. It wasn't a dream. He was in the flesh. I stood mesmerised for about what felt like a year. He walked between everyone and walked passed me. I nearly jumped on him, but managed to restrain myself. I could feel the hairs coming out from under my T-shirt. The fan in me nearly escaped. On my lips were 'Can I have your autograph please?' I was only stopped when I saw his security man behind him who was carrying an M16. I thought I had no chance of getting picked because there was a lot of big looking guys there, but to my shock I was tapped on the shoulder. I was picked along with nine others. Everyone else was paid $20 for turning out and offered the opportunity to stay on set to watch the filming. We all jumped into his four-wheel jeeps with his bodyguards and were driven to his mobile home up on the set. I sat in a big room with the others while Stallone got changed and put on some make-up. Half an hour later he emerged, shook our hands and introduced himself. He needed no introduction. He gave us the gist of the story in full secrecy and later we had to sign a contract making us liable to prosecution should we release any information about the film. I then spent most of the day with him doing main shots for the film. After twelve hours filming we were given a four-wheel drive between five of us and keys to some rooms in the same hotel as Stallone. I showered, changed and ate a fabulous five star meal. It was all paid for.

To top it all I was also getting paid $50 per day, which wasn't bad. I did this for about three weeks and in that time became very close friends with Stallone. He took a shining to Scottie, who joined me on set after I got him a job, along with myself and a few selected others. When the filming of extras finished he asked a few of us to stay on with him as personal friends. I did this for the next four weeks. It was the greatest experience of my life. I slept in one of the rooms next to him which he had rented at King Solomon Hotel. He rented the whole top floor. I went

To be someone was a wonderful thing

wherever he went. I ate at the same table as him. I went to studios with him. I was almost his shadow. I almost even pissed with him in the toilet. He enjoyed the company of Scottie and I because we were not full of shit. We were down to earth. We did not revolve around money. We didn't have much! That's what he loved.

One afternoon we were all sitting in his apartment when he switched on the television. On the screen was a helicopter. When we looked closer it was coming towards the hotel we were in. It was being filmed from the rooftop directly above us. I thought 'what the hell is going on?' His main security adviser, an ex-Vietnam veteran, on one million dollars a year was proving a point to him. This all happened because a fundamentalist Arab leader had issued a death threat against Stallone because he was feeding U.S. dollars into the Jewish state. This exercise was to prove how easy it would be to kill him.

Anyway, this helicopter hovered above our heads on the roof. By now we were watching it on the screen. Minutes later his main man attached himself to the side of the building and absailed down to our window. Seconds later he came smashing through the hotel window to land within a foot of Stallone. I was totally gobsmacked. I honestly though it was part of another film. But this was for real and I shit myself instantly. This was not a game. This was serious shit. He expected his bodyguards to take the bullet should one be fired at him. In a sense I agreed because they got paid a lot of money to protect him. Security was upgraded right away. The whole top floor was re-windowed at the expense of the hotel. It cost sixty-thousand dollars. The glass was bullet proof and about an inch thick. The hotel was watertight. No-one got near the top floor. Orders were shoot to kill. Luckily Scottie and I were well known. We could come and go as we pleased. I am sure his body guards hated the treatment we received. I could see it in their eyes.

On one other occasion Stallone, Scottie, his body guards and myself all sat having a few drinks in King Solomon's private bar. Stallone stood and said he was going out to a pub for a few quiet drinks with Scottie and myself – minus his bodyguards. He borrowed a long overcoat, a baseball cap and some shades from his bodyguards and told them to be there when he got back. He was advised not to go out on his own, but he told them to shut up. When he had dressed up you would have never known it was him. We were just three guys out for a few beers. We visited a good few bars and shared intimate parts of our life. Stallone mentioned his separation from Brigette Neilson saying that you win some you lose some. 'What's a few million bucks?' he remarked. We did this a few times. I felt he was being suffocated at times and needed an escape. He said 'its great being famous, but you also have to accept arseholes with the package'.

On another occasion, at the end of filming, before we all parted they held this huge party for all the stars, directors, producers – all the major components in making the film possible. Scottie and myself were also invited. We had talked to Stallone about hiring a suit for the occasion. He said 'don't do it for me. Come as you are'. So we did. We put on our best jeans and shirts and off we went. We left slightly earlier, to go for a few drinks in another bar as a few friends were leaving the next day. We had a few drinks and said our goodbye's. We then headed for the disco where the function was being held. Stallone had not arrived yet, but was due any minute. As we approached the doors we were stopped by a bouncer who we didn't know. We said 'we were invited'. He asked for the invite, but we didn't have it, because we had been verbally invited. We asked to see the manager. We explained that we were friends of Stallone's, but he thought we were bullshitting him. He still refused to let us in and told his bouncers to get rid of us before we caused a scene. Just at that moment Stallone turned up in his jeep. As we were being pushed out of the way he enquired where were we going. We said that the manager had refused us entry. Stallone went mad. 'You refuse entry to my friends because of their appearance you weasel! I have a good mind to cancel the party'. The manager shit himself. 'I do apologise, the drinks are on me all evening, come in, come in'. With that we entered with Stallone. As I passed the manager I called him a fucking dickhead. I made him eat humblepie all evening. It was great watching him grovel all evening.

Stallone was leaving the very next morning for America to finish shooting the film. Before he left he said we could continue to stay in the hotel suite for another four days as it was paid for. Which we did. It was

To be someone was a wonderful thing

fabulous. We had food on tap, beer on draught, and the use of all the facilities. Unfortunately we knew this would all come to an end very soon. One good thing apart from the experience of it was that Stallone had given us a cheque for a tidy amount of money. This would see us alright for at least a few months.

It was the experience of a lifetime. An experience I shall never forget.

Three weeks later and I was back on the Kibbutz. I was ready to go home, but I had no home. The first leg of my travels were nearly over. I had one last spending spree in Tel-Aviv before I flew home. I must have spent about a thousand dollars in a week. I had a fabulous time. It was well earned.

I had a few dilemmas with going home. I didn't want to go and live with any of my family. My only chance was to live with Ian in his bedsit which he had moved into. One other opportunity was to try and get the unit to sort something out.

I thought 'sod it I'll cross that bridge when I come to it'. I booked my ticket home for the 22nd of December 1988 from Tel-Aviv.

As I was leaving I wondered whether Bonnie Scotland had changed? My answer was – I bet not!

Chapter Seventeen

Going Home

I flew into Gatwick at 9pm. It was snowing heavily and the winds were gale force. The plane touched down and in the process skidded about 200 metre's off the runway. I swore I heard the captain's heartbeat. Fear was in everyone's eyes. I was loving every minute of it. People sat praying to God. Others were lighting small temples for the Buddha and looking to the ghosts of Dacca in their deep sub-conscious minds, only to find that moments later they had been saved by the expertise of the pilot. Not by the hand of God or whoever. When we finally stopped, the religion disappeared and the fear left by the rear exit. As people disembarked there were many choice words used to describe the captain. I thanked him for a nice flight. He said 'Cheers', in a Jewish accent.

I spent that evening in the train station as my train was not due until 7.30am next morning. Train stations are funny places. They are the homes for many people – until they are moved on of course. We live in a strange society. We have the insatiable habit of not allowing people worse off than ourselves a night's kip on a dirty floor. We'd rather see them on the street. As long as we are alright. I had learned a few things while travelling. Although cultures are different, one permanent issue lies engraved in the Western World and that is selfishness. We walk past people on the streets. If we are approached we condemn them. Even I do it. I am conditioned to do it. I needed to think about this because at that moment in time I was homeless. I condemned myself. I need to do better for myself. I boarded the train for the city after a long night thinking about who I was.

On my arrival I booked my rucksack into left luggage and decided to go to the local D.S.S. office to see what they could offer me. I went in and went through the usual degrading stuff that they throw at you. What a

Going Home

hassle to get £29 per week! I wondered if I would get a Christmas bonus in my giro.

My aunt worked there, the one I lived with when I was in the Sea Cadets. When she saw me she enquired what I had been up to and all that. I told her about my travels and that I had nowhere to stay. With that she offered me a bed until I got myself sorted out. I had fallen on my feet again. I collected my rucksack and moved in. My aunt said it was no problem to stay there as long as I wanted. So I did. I visited my mates, especially Ian and the unit.

I began looking for a job. I got work as a doorman at a Cafe'-bar on the main street called 'Ici' – means here is. I was on two hundred pounds a week and worked five days from 2pm until midnight. I loved the work. I met loads of people and made new friends. You would not believe the perks of being a doorman. I worked there for about six months. I had a few fights and was offered money to have paid by both men and women. I also worked as a personal chauffeur for the boss's friends and made loads of money.

The job certainly had many perks. I remember on one occasion I was invited to a party in an exclusive area west of the city. I was not due to finish work until midnight. This was alright because it wasn't starting until after then. Mark, a bouncer I worked alongside, was going to the party with me.

We arrived at the house and was met at the door by the hostess who was a lovely middle-aged woman. She showed us inside to where it was all happening. To our surprise nearly everyone was female and almost naked. She turned to us and said 'If you want to stay you'll have to get undressed'. With that she undid her dress and walked into the party. To my amazement nobody even looked at us. Mark said 'lets go for it'. I was a little more shy than he was, but eventually I got undressed.

It was like being in a nudist camp. I had been to one when I was in Israel. Well, by mistake really! The story goes like this. I had paid to go on to a private beach. There were two entry points, one for the nudist beach and the other for the normal beach. I went through the wrong entry point. I had also paid the extra few shequels for the nudist beach, although at the time I had questioned it as I thought it was expensive for a normal beach. As I walked through the entry point something was not right. People had nothing on. At first it was rather strange. As I walked amongst all the people I received a few glances of 'get your shorts off'. A few minutes later I was on the sand face down with my shorts off. My arse was facing the sky. That day I got badly sunburnt on my arse as I did not move until it was time to go. The next day I returned to the same beach and made sure I went onto the normal beach. I was not ready for full nudity yet. In a sense I was very aware of my body. I felt I was chubby for my size.

Anyway, back to the party. I had undressed, but I was not so comfortable. Mark on the other hand was 'getting in there'. He was dancing with a couple of the women who were there. On average they all must have been about thirty-five years old. He was loving it. I on the other hand headed for the drinks and a secluded spot near the swimming pool in the conservatory. Leading from the room where the party was. I sat there in a daze as women's' bodies passed me heading for the pool. The few men who were there seemed to be very busy entertaining the women. The women were also entertaining other women. This was my first contact with lesbianism.

A few minutes later the hostess came over to me and said 'you don't have to be shy here. We're all having fun, and we all share each other'. I said 'that it was first time I had been to this type of party'. She told me to come with her to show me something. With that I followed her through another room which led to a staircase to the bedrooms. We entered a bedroom which was empty. We sat on the bed and drank some champagne. After about ten minutes she asked if I wanted to have some fun, to which I replied 'yeah'. We lay on the bed touching each other when suddenly the door opened and a three women entered. They all got onto the bed and began to fondle the two of us. I was not to keen on this as two of the women began to get a little rough with me. I managed to get off the bed and head towards my pile of clothes in the hall. I had had enough. I looked for Mark on my way out but he was surrounded by women on the floor. He seemed to be enjoying himself. He was drowning

Going Home

in sex. What a way to drown!! I got out of the house and flagged a taxi down. I got home and went to bed.

The next day I arrived for work to find Mark covered in scratches and bruises. He asked where I had gone. I told him I had left early. He said he wished he had too. He said that after about an hour of fun he was dragged into a bedroom with the hostess who had invited three women into the room also. After they had sex he was tied to the bed while they all went mad. He said they were like fucking lunatics. They had all gone sadistically mad. He was the lamb on the spit.

That next evening the hostess came into the club and invited us both to another party, which we declined. We also decided to show her the front door and banned her from the club.

I was invited to another party by a friend of Mark. We arrived there after work at twelve-thirty to find the party over. Everyone was pissed out of their heads. We asked where the beer was and were pointed in the direction of the bathroom. In the bathroom were two cans of shitty beer. We took both cans and sat in the midst of the drunken haze for about the time it took to drink them both. We left rather pissed off. That was the last party we went to thrown by friends off Mark.

A few times when I was on the door I was given twenty Pound notes with names and addresses on them, by both men and women. Most of the times I would not take up the offer and give it back – at other times I would keep the money.

Being a doorman can be quite stressful at times. You are a wanted sexual commodity. Everyone wants to have the doorman. This statement is two-sided though. Women want the doorman for pleasure while men in most cases want to have a go at the doorman. In this instance a doorman has the upperhand because he is sober.

I remember on one occasion when I was working in a club. It was a Saturday and we were packed out the door. There were four bouncers on that night. I was on the front door with a guy called Graham. We both got on really well. It must have been about ten 'o' clock when this guy came out of the club pissed out of his head. He had managed to sneak a glass out of the club under his jacket. As he walked away he produced the

Going Home

glass and began to laugh at us saying this was our glass and he was keeping it. We told him to be on his way and out of our face. A few minutes later he returned with the glass waving around in his hand and saying he was going back into the club. I told the guy that he was not going anywhere near the door. To this he replied that he worked for the Ministry of Defence. As he got nearer the threat of being glassed by some drunken guy was facing me. As I stood on the step of the front door I unfastened my suit jacket button so I could respond rather quickly in case he tried anything. After another few minutes I got fed up bartering with this guy and decided to sort him out. In one fell swoop, and in a matter of about one second, I had hit this guy full in the face with my fist and was back on the step fastening my jacket button before he even hit the ground. No-one saw it as it was so fast. Even Graham who was standing next to me saw very little except for the movement of a black suit. As the guy hit the floor I heard a thud. I think that was his nose on the concrete. He was out cold. We stood there and wondered what had happened. 'Did he fall over?' we said to people who came to his aid – we never saw a thing, just this guy on the floor. A few minutes later he was taken away by ambulance to the hospital.

A few hours later we got a phone call from a distressed mother complaining that her son had received a broken nose, a broken cheek bone, had lost four teeth, had a bruised eye and a burst lip. Apparently she was a high – up member of the city's council committee.

The manager came to see me about the incident which I said I knew nothing about. The other bouncers said the same. It was a tight community of bouncers. Everyone knew that you got arseholes who at times deserved a good punch in the face. This guy was one.

On one other occasion, again a night when we were packed out of the door, a girl came to me several times complaining of being harassed by another girl. She pointed her out to me. I went over and had a quiet word with her, asking what was going on. This girl knew nothing of the incident and said that the other girl was shit-stirring. Minutes later the girl was back at me complaining again. This time I went to the girl and asked if she would move seats so she was not in the way of this other girl. The girl was

Going Home

happy with this but her boyfriend was not. He stood up and said 'we're not moving so fuck off'. With that I said 'Right you're both leaving by the back door. Move it'. Just as I said that he punched me right in the face. He had caught me off-guard. Luckily it was not too hard a punch for me not to recover and respond quickly. In a split second I had punched the guy several times and was in the process of dragging him out the back door. What I did not allow for was that this guy was part of a ruthless gang. One other thing I did not know was that there were about forty of them sitting in the club. When they saw this going on they went absolutely mad. The place erupted. Chairs were being thrown across the room. Glasses were thrown at anyone who got in the way and people began to fight each other. It was a mess. Within a few minutes the police had arrived to sort it out. It was about twenty minutes before it all calmed down. Everyone was asked to leave the club as it was closing. The manager could not believe his eyes. His club was ruined. He called in some emergency furnishers would could sort out the club ready for opening the next evening. Again he came to me and asked what the hell had gone on. This time I told him it was because of some shit-stirring tart.

The next evening we opened as planned. It must have been about eight 'o' clock. I was at the front door sorting out the cloakroom tickets when suddenly for guys rushed in and began to punch and kick me. I managed to get a few good punches to two or three of them before getting a hold of the guy who had punched me the night before. He had came back for revenge, but was so far getting beat. As I was fighting off these guys a few of them stood back because of the fight I was putting up. Finally I stood 'saying come on them you arseholes let's go again'. They walked away saying they would return with more guys. They did not return that evening.

A few nights later the guy returned on his own. I again stood my ground, but this time he had not come to fight. He had come to sort out this mess. We had a chat and he bought me a few drinks. He did say to me that he had never met anyone so aggressive and determined to fight back in his life. He said he would like to have me on his side if a fight broke out.

Going Home

After this I saw him a couple of times, but we had no problems anymore.

After that job I worked as a hairdresser, but found it cheap labour. I did it for about six months. All in all I had a good laugh pampering the women and all that false shit that goes with it. I also formed a relationship with the owner's sister. This was doomed to fail right from the start. I was young and enjoying life. I was forewarned about work and pleasure, but did not heed the advice. I had to learn for myself. This was my first major relationship. Working in the hairdressers also had a few perks.

On one occasion I was asked to wash a lady's hair. Which I did. The sinks we used to wash hair were positioned in such a way that the lady had to lie with the back of her neck resting on a groove in the sink. This meant that the lady's face was looking up to the ceiling, or in some cases your face as you were washing their hair. As I was washing her hair I noticed she had undone her blouse so I could see right down her cleavage. She was not wearing a bra. As I continued to wash her hair, she asked if I would like to fondle her tits, to which I replied I was not paid to feel tits. She then said that she would pay me if I wanted her to. I again said no thanks. After washing her hair she continued to flirt with me and on the way out slipped me her address on a piece of paper.

She used to come in every week and ask for me to wash her hair. Every week she would show me her breasts. The offer was still there. One day I decided to take up her up on the offer and meet her in the evening for a few drinks. I met her in a pub not far from where I worked. We had a few drinks and went back to her place. This was one of my first encounters with sex: safe sex that is. It wasn't what I thought it would be. In the films it had been portrayed as being fabulous and the greatest experience in the world. I was still waiting for something to happen. It never did...!! I left later that night feeling like a tart. I had broken the first rule of my life, one man one women. In all my time as a bouncer, I had not broken that rule, but finally temptation had got the better of me. Why I did this I will never know.

After this flirtation the woman continued to want me, but I never went again. She continued to show her breasts though.

Going Home

My career as a hairdresser came to an abrupt end after a hectic week of cock-ups with people's hair. I had managed to burn one lady's hair with a pair of tongs. Another had been dyed the wrong colour. One guy's hair I had cut too short and he was fuming. This all came to a head on the Friday. Marilyn, the girl I was friendly with had asked me do something and not to get it wrong. Which I did. She went mad. So I told her to fuck off in a packed salon in front of all her ladies and the juniors. That was it. It was all over. I left that moment and never looked back. It was an horrendous experience for me. I felt a huge weight lift from my shoulders as I journeyed home that evening.

I went back to working in the clubs. I got a buzz from being on the door. I loved the job. Because I was only working from 8.00pm until 2am, I needed a day job to occupy my time. So I successfully applied for work as a sorter/driver in the Post Office.

By this time I was planning my next trip for early March 1990. I had itchy feet for travelling and had to scratch them. I was heading for Australia and the Far East. I began reading the book again. My bible for travelling around the world. I saved up £2000 and applied for my visa. I got it a few weeks later.

I was working all the hours I could. It was only a matter of time and I would be off again.

Before I knew it I was on my travels once more. After a weepie goodbye with Ian with whom I had been in care and my aunt and uncle with whom I had stayed for nearly a year and a bit. I had definitely outstayed my welcome. I had thoughts of not going as the train pulled away, but I knew I had to. I had a long journey ahead of me but I was used to that by now. On the train I looked back at what had happened over the past thirteen months at home. I'd had lots of fun in the clubs and with the lads – Ian, Simon and George, Ian's brother.

One thing I did not miss was the continual squabbling within my family. They would never change. They would always be the Rileys.

I was now in the frame of mind where I could not give a shit. I was thinking about myself not other people – was this being a selfish bastard or what? No, not really this was about me. So sod them!

Going Home

Again I had left behind some psychological baggage; actually more than I thought. I felt lighter and healthier as I moved on. It was a healing process for me.

I flew from Gatwick and arrived in Darwin three weeks later. Yes three weeks! Well I did stop over in Bali for two days then went up to Bangkok by bus. The bus trip was horrendous. I shared a seat with a box of chickens. It was a nightmare. I spent most of my time on the beaches and eating Thai food in Phuket, a resort not far from Bangkok. I travelled up North up to Chaing Mai where I worked in some paddy fields with a small community of Buddhist's. I stayed there for nearly a week which was enough to almost blow my mind. In a sense I had been searching the world for one true religion and belief. This was part of my exploration. I quiet liked the Zen Buddhist way of life and their philosophies. We smoked some sort of healing compound every day before and after work. It was supposed to ward of evil spirits and cleanse the body. What it did for me was to get me stoned out of my head. I learned about their culture, how they see life and how they bring up their children. This was of particular interest to me. In the West, everything was so different!

It was a culture shock for me. We had nothing, not even toilets or electricity. We only had each other, our meditation and the environment. Nothing else mattered in this village. The family was the focus of all life; if we had no family, then we had nothing.

I then travelled to Singapore, Jakarta and back to Bali.

Chapter Eighteen
The Land of Opportunity

I loved the Far East. The way of life was so easy. While there I met people from America and Europe with no plans of ever returning to their native country. They spent most of their days dealing on the black market-dollars and drugs with the odd dabble in prostitution. This was what the Americans had left behind: the remnants of Western exploitation.

I then flew on to Darwin. I stayed in a Backpackers' hostel in Darwin until I has established some contacts and exchanged some addresses. At that time there was not much happening in the way of work, so I decided to have a look around and to take it easy.

I met up with a guy from Oxford and a girl from London. One day we went to have a look around at some nearby beaches. You have to be careful in Darwin as it is known for its crocodile population. We arrived at this sandy beach that went on for miles. We sat down and prepared for a day on the beach. Ten minutes later we saw a four – wheel jeep driving towards us on the sand. It was the coast guard. When he reached us a guy jumped out of the jeep and told us to move off the beach as there was a twenty-foot crocodile on the loose. Just as he said that an Aborigine man came out the bush with two sticks. He was banging them together. Suddenly he was off. About twenty feet from us, the crocodile appeared. The Aborigine and the jeep headed towards the crocodile. The crocodile made a run towards us but was blocked by the Aborigine who was taunting it with the sticks. A few seconds later a net was thrown over it and the Aborigine was on top of the crocodile trying to wire its mouth so it could not bite anyone. He also managed to wire its tail to its body so it could not do any damage with it. This happened in about the space of a few minutes. I stood shell shocked as the jeep drove off with the crocodile strapped to

The Land of Opportunity

the trailer on the back. I had only been in Australia about two days and I was already wondering what the hell I was doing in the place.

I left Darwin a few days later and travelled into the bush and onto Perth. The bus trip took three days. It wasn't a bad trip as the buses have really good air conditioning and television, etc. I stayed in Perth for a few days before moving on to Fremantle. In a short time I had started work in a small chemical factory as a storeman/fork lift driver. Fremantle is a fabulous small town full of Italian restaurants and cafe bars. In Fremantle I lived in a youth hostel called Freo 200. There were about one hundred people living there. You got your own bedroom and shared a kitchen, living room and bathroom. The good thing about Freo 200 was that there were plenty of people to get to know. I soon formed a few relationships with some guys called Jason, Saj, Matt, Scott, Kevin and Big Al. Scott and Matt were from Melbourne whilst all the rest were from England. We spent most of our time in the cafes drinking Redback – a wheat beer from Western Australia. In a short while I was getting into a rut. Work, drink, work and drink. I was fed up with it.

After about four months I managed to get thrown out of Freo 200 along with all the other guys for being pissed as farts one night. We were all so drunk that we were running along the halls shouting and screaming, keeping everyone up all night.

We all moved into the hostel across the road called Bundia. It was a great hostel but again this was not to last. I sought more adventure.

I moved onto Kalgoorlie, a big mining town about six hours east of Perth. It was very expensive to live there because of the gold mining. I planned to live in the local campsite and had borrowed a tent from Matt. On this part of my travels I was with a guy called Malcolm. It was not very easy getting a job either. It took me a few days to get one but again I was in the right place at the right time.

I met this guy in a pub. He was a prospector. He asked if I would help him dig his plot of land in return for food and 25% of any gold he found. I agreed to do so. I left the next morning with another guy whom I had met on the campsite. I began working for this prospector. He paid me very little and worked me very hard. After about two weeks of digging

The Land of Opportunity

with a pick axe and shovel I gave up. He pleaded for me to stay but I needed to earn more money.

I left him digging his patch of land and started working for Boulder Drilling as a offsider. This entailed working on land drilling rig which drilled for samples for geologists to sift through for Gold etc.

Three days after starting my new job I heard my prospector had struck gold loads of it. As a matter of fact loads of it. What a life eh! You win some you lose some!

On my next trip to Kalgoorlie I saw him in a pub celebrating. He saw me alright though. But just think, I could have made a fortune. Is that Sod's law or what? I was gutted.

I worked for about three months as an offsider until Christmas. I had made about $3000 dollars. I spent a week in Kalgoorlie which cost me about $1500 on beer alone. I had a great time but my liver began to feel it, so I moved on.

I left Kalgoorlie and headed back to Perth to meet up with the guys I had met in Fremantle. We were planning to go to Melbourne between Christmas and New Year. We all chipped in an hundred dollars to buy a cheap car. When I say cheap, I mean cheap. It was a Toyota and it was registered for 1964. It was a heap and we were suckered into buying it.

Jason, Kevin and I began our two thousand mile journey on the 26th of December. We planned to get to Matt's house for New Year. We got about a thousand miles, and were right in the middle of the Nullabor when we blew a piston. The nearest garage was about two hundred kilometres away. By this time all three of us were dehydrated, skint, rather hot, and absolutely pissed off. We were in the middle of nowhere. Who would stop for three crazed looking nutjobs? I wouldn't. It got rather frightening when Jason began to hallucinate with sun stroke. Kevin and I lay underneath the car out of the sun. The temperature was about 38_C. In other words, fucking hot. Hot enough to fry eggs for breakfast on the bonnet of the car.

The time 6pm, the place nowhere. It had been two days since breaking down and only one bus had passed us. It was new Years Eve. Who would be travelling over the Nullabor on this day of any? No-one! By now I was

The Land of Opportunity

really shitting myself. We were all in bad shape and consciousness kept slipping away.

Luckily a truck driver stopped to give us water. This was only the second vehicle we had seen in two days. We drank about five litres of water in the space of seconds. It was a God send. The truck driver radioed forward and we received assistance about an hour later. We were given plenty to eat and drink and taken to Adelaide – almost a day's drive. It cost us nothing. Saying that, we spent New Year under the chassis of an old Toyota. What a year.

We made up for it the week after. We spent a few days in Adelaide then moved onto Melbourne, where we celebrated a late New Year.

Melbourne was fabulous. I spent three weeks there. I went to the Australian Tennis Open, to see Deacon Blue, Simple Minds and U2. It was great, but my money was rapidly running out, and I had no plans to work anymore.

Chapter Nineteen
On Deaths Doorstep

I moved again. I passing through Sydney on my way up to Surfers Paradise. I spent a lot of lying on the beach and swimming in The Great Barrier Reef with the dolphins. From there I went by four-wheel drive to Cape Tribulation and back to Sydney. I had a great time.

About this time I was beginning to feel run-down. I had a sudden thirst. When I got to Sydney I was easily drinking about six or seven litres of liquid a day. This prompted me to become even more ill which I did. I, at first spent most of my days in the hostel drinking coke, but then diet drinks because normal coke was to sweet. Whenever I drank anything, usually about two litres of juice in three minutes, I would spend the next two hours going to the toilet every ten minutes until I needed another drink.

By this time I had been ill in Sydney for about a week and had lost two stone in weight. I decided to see a doctor. He said I had a flu bug and that I should continue to eat and drink loads. How could I, I had stopped eating a week ago. Food was not staying down. I tried to eat and drink. I drank a pint of milk which curdled in my stomach and came up a few days later as solid lumps of cream. This in turn tore a small hole in my lung which caused me to have problems with breathing: another addition to my flu bug.

Two days later I was totally fucked I went to see another doctor, to get a second opinion. I was rushed to the hospital as soon as he checked my urine. He knew his job . He was on the ball. I am sure he used my sugared urine for his coffee. My urine was 100% sugar. I couldn't afford an ambulance – AU$75 so I took a taxi for AU$3. As a traveller it was the natural choice. You know me by now 'its cheap so it'll do me!'

On Deaths Doorstep

As we approached the casualty department I remember becoming very faint. I opened the door and instead of getting my bag and paying the driver, I hit concrete. That's all I remember. A porter later told me that the driver dragged me out of the car, threw my bag on top of me and drove off. He didn't even wait to be paid. I suppose he thought I had Aids or was a drug addict.

Anyway, I woke up in Intensive Care one day later. I went into a coma in the taxi. I had a few drips in my arms, a resuscitation machine keeping me alive, and an insulin pendulum slowly feeding me insulin. When I first woke, all I saw was a hazy white something. Heaven entered my head. Death was on my lips until this human face half scared me to bloody death. At that moment I knew my judgement day was again postponed.

I spent four weeks in hospital in Sydney recovering. I was told I was lucky to be alive. I readily accepted that. I went through some intense counselling for my diabetes, which enabled me to come to terms with it quicker. The choice was either to look after myself or die. I choose to live. Wouldn't you?

They sat that Australia is the Land of Opportunity. I say differently. Visiting Australia, the Great Barrier Reef, Sydney and the Opera House, visiting Alice Springs and Ayers Rock, sun bathing on Bondi Beach and boating around the islands of the Queensland coast was fabulous. But in reality they have a tremendously high level of drugs, a prostitution level they cannot control, areas which have become no-go places after a certain time at night. Their crime levels have soared due to high unemployment. I could go on with an endless list. It is by no means the Land of Opportunity. I did enjoy myself but I had no plans to stay and settle there.

I left Australia in a sad state and went back to live at my aunt's in the city and come to terms with my change in lifestyle. It wasn't too drastic for me and I quickly got into the routine. The food side was no problem because I ate healthily anyway and wasn't keen on sugary foods. I had to start life again. I found the motivation from somewhere. Maybe my mother is watching over me and inspiring me to live on after all.

Chapter Twenty

A real job

After I had settled back I began to pursue my interest in Social Work. When I was in Australia I had written a report of my experiences in care and had sent a copy to my officer in charge. So when I returned I contacted him and his wife whom he had married a few years previously and had been Social Work manager when I was in care. It was mentioned in a few pieces of literature connected with Social Work and was also discussed at some Social Work committee meetings for child care.

I contacted the Social Services relief pool and was interviewed for a temporary job in the relief pool on an assessment basis. I began work in a Day Centre. It was a centre for adults with disabilities. I was initially there for two weeks to see what my capabilities were. Within the two weeks they were so impressed that I stayed on for another year.

At that time I was only twenty-one, but my maturity began to show through. Shortly after being moved several times, within the relief pool, I was interviewed for a full time job at the centre, which I got.

My job was as a Day Centre Officer. I was involved in assessing clients for their suitability at the centre, visiting them at home, doing work to bring the family into the centre so they might participate and understand their relative's disability and assessing them in various workshops – art, cooking, woodwork, picture framing, computer programming and reading and writing. I had to write up reports, assessments, day sheets, admissions and discharges. I was in at the deep end and I loved it. I was hooked on Social Work. I believe you either love it or hate it. There is no in-between.

A few months later I was again interviewed for a unique community care project which was well ahead of its time. Actually two years to be

A real job

precise. Anyway, I got the job. My job was to integrate adults who had spent long terms in institutions back into their own community and also to assess the facilities available in their own area so that they might use them.

Initially this would have worked. But as always in Social Work there were a few problems. Another worker, Odile was her name, and myself had a case load of thirty, all of whom lived in areas other than that in which the centre was located. They had also become very institutionalised and had very different needs, many of which could not be met by us. Some could cope on their own, but others had no chance. My task was mammoth. In theory it could be achieved, but in practice it was a non-starter. I did it for about four months and requested a move back to the other Day Centre. I was receiving little support or back up and felt very isolated at times.

All decisions had to be made from there. I had no autonomy. The annoying thing was that I was accountable for results. I needed to show that what I was doing was worth the money allocated to the project. I managed this part quite well. I loved the work and the challenge, but I also needed supervision and support, none of which I received.

Back at the Day Centre things were not too good. We had some staff changes and the team was going through a back-stabbing stage. Staff were talking about colleagues behind their backs. With one member of staff who you could guarantee that if you wanted your manager to know something, all you had to do was to tell them. I think every staff team possibly has one. I hadn't become unhappy with social work itself only with the politics of social work. They were everywhere. They even stopped you doing the job the right way sometimes; all because some person in a high-up place thought they could do the job hands-on better than you could. If they can, then get them down here for some role modelling was my reply.

Then of course you've got a manager. My manager was at times very devious. At every staff meeting there would be a hidden agenda. My manager would have all the decisions mapped out before they were even discussed. So much for being a client run centre! So much for team spirit

A real job

and all that shit. Even though my manager was in fact quite good at some things. My manager could get you to do something which at first you did not want to do with great ease.

During this time I had gone on holiday to Tenerife with Ian, with whom I had been in care. We had a great time and I fell in love with a Manchester girl called Zoe. It was love at first site. We spent a fabulous week together. I was only there a week, Zoe was there for two. Our departing was a sad occasion because I knew we lived three-hundred and fifty miles apart.

I flew home with an address and memories of a great week. One bad thing that lingered in my gut was the stories you hear of holiday romances: that they never work. I somehow knew that our relationship was different.

It was six hours on the train from Glasgow. We had flown to Glasgow. As soon as I got home I wrote her a letter her. I told everyone about her, and they were sick to death hearing about her. She was definitely different. I knew it would work.

I commuted for several weeks by train to be with Zoe. I remember our first meeting after the holiday. I got off the train to meet Zoe at the station entrance. I had never been to Manchester before and had only heard of Moss Side on the news. As I walked towards the exit I had a severe case of butterflies. I kept wandering what I would do if it didn't work out.

A few weeks later I was invited to spend Christmas with Zoe and her family. We would go back up North for New Year. I really enjoyed being there and felt accepted by her family. I really felt wanted. I got on incredibly well with her mum and dad, always one of the crucial elements in any relationship. You need good in-laws.

After New Year, Zoe returned to Manchester. We phoned each other every day. I visited several times until about mid March that year. The strain of travelling and being apart was affecting both of us. It was make or break time. A decision had to be made regarding our long term relationship.

In a lucky sort of way my contract at work was coming to an end and was about to be renewed. I really wanted a change of job, another area of Social Work. So I didn't renew my contract.

A real job

My move into child care would prove a difficult one, principally because I was still quite close to the care system. I was only twenty-one years old. I needed to move to another city. Not only because of work, but because family issues had emerged again. I was getting webbed into the world of the Rileys.

I chatted to Zoe and her parents about the possibility of moving to Manchester to find work and to start afresh. They thought it was a great idea. So off I went. This time I was not looking back. I dumped all my bad luggage, wrote off my relatives, and settled into my new family very quickly.

Within two months of taking it easy and working for Zoe's dad, I managed to find work in an adolescents' unit with Catholic Children's Rescue Society in Manchester. I'm still there and I really like the work, being and fully committed to the young people in our care. I work in a well established staff team and a reasonably well run unit.

Finally, I have reached another height in my life's ambitions. I am doing a job I originally set out to get many years ago.

In September 1992 I proposed to Zoe, who accepted. We were married the year after. I have a really good relationship with all of her family and am seen not as a son-in-law, but as a son. This responsibility I take very seriously.

Unfortunately my relationship with my aunt has been severed due to family squabbles.

I think it all stemmed from when we got engaged. We went up North to break the news to my aunt and uncle, whom I almost saw as my mother and father. On our arrival my aunt advised me to visit my father as he had been asking about me. I took the good advice and went with Zoe to see him. He was living at my grandmother's house. In a sense I needed to see if he had changed. I needed to see him for myself. I had to face the music sometime. I needed to say what I felt about him.

When we arrived at my grandmother's my father was on the floor pissed out of his head. Nothing had changed – he was still pissed and my grandmother still moaned about this and that. I stayed in the house about twenty minutes. It got to the stage when he was taking the piss out of

A real job

Zoe, for her accent. Had I not left quickly I would have killed him, so we hurried away. When we got out of the house I broke down and cried. That was the end. That was all I needed.

On my return to my aunt's she became annoyed that I had visited my father. But it was her idea! I am always on the losing end when it comes to my family. It didn't matter now, I had a new family. A caring and loving family.

Our next visit up North was another mess. Zoe's parents and younger sister accompanied us this time. I invited my officer in charge and his wife so we could all meet before the wedding, my aunt's idea again . This was one piece of advice I was about to regret forever.

The actual visit went very well, but I could sense something was not right. We left, but our goodbye was not the same. Something had happened. I do not know what! I left saying I would phone soon.

Things were beginning to roll very fast. The months were speeding by. Our wedding plans were in place. I had decided not to invite any of my family to the wedding, except my aunt and uncle, and a few other relatives on my mother's side.

I had also changed my name by deed-pole to my mother's maiden name. I had totally disinherited my whole family. Its a decision I made on my own for the better.

It must have been six weeks before I picked up the phone to contact my aunt after our visit. I had been very busy. She hadn't contacted me either for whatever reason. She had a phone and knew my number. Anyway when I did, phone, I received the cold shoulder. The call was abrupt and she didn't want to know me. I phoned my uncle the day after, still suffering from the shock of being pushed away, and was told to figure it out myself. I could not understand it as I had no contact with my family except my mum's sister Moira whom I was quite close to.

As the wedding approached, I sent invites to my aunt and uncle and her family receiving apologies from everyone except my aunt. I was totally gutted. I was devastated. What had I done that was so bad?

On the 12th September 1992, regardless of all the hassle, we got married and had a fabulous day without the various people who had not

A real job

come. I feel that they would have only caused problems anyway. Zoe and I really enjoy life together. Now and again I pause for a second to think about my aunt, but that's all it is a pause. I feel she has a lot of work to do within her own life now. She has to work it out because I can't.

Zoe is expecting our first child on February 8th 1994. We cannot wait. I don't think her mother and father can either.

I still see my officer in charge and his wife they are the best friends I have. They are, as a matter of fact, family.

I still get pissed with Ian when I go up North or he comes down to Manchester. Our relationship has grown stronger.

I don't see my mum's sister anymore. I feel I only went there because she was the closest thing to my mother. I now realise that I am the closest thing to my mother . I have her in my heart and in my memories. She will always be with me.